HN
90
.M3
1988

MASS COMMUNICATION AND INTERNATIONAL POLITICS

A Case Study of Press Reactions to the 1973 Arab-Israeli War

Alan Jay Zaremba
Northeastern University

Sheffield Publishing Company
Salem, Wisconsin

For information about this book, write or call:
Sheffield Publishing Company
P.O. Box 359
Salem, Wisconsin 53168
(414) 843-2281

Copyright © 1988 by Alan Jay Zaremba

ISBN 0-88133-386-7

All rights reserved. No part of this book may be reproduced, stored in a retrieval system, or transmitted in any form or by any means without permission in writing from the publisher.

Printed in the United States of America

for

Meyer and Helen Zaremba

and

Dr. Molefi Kete Asante

Contents

1. Introduction — 1
   a discussion of the nature of the study in terms of the region's global significance

2. Methodology — 5
   a description of the procedure used to analyze the media content. Illustrations are used to explain the quantitative and qualitative aspects of the study.

3. *The New York Times* — 11
   excerpts from the *New York Times* and discussion of the *New York Times'* reaction to aspects of the conflict. Specifically, the following issues are addressed. Aggression, Terrorism, Land Legitimacy, Culpability, Intransigence, Superpower Culpability, and issues surrounding the use of oil as a diplomatic weapon.

4. *The Moscow News* — 39
   chapters 4-8 follow the structure employed in chapter 3. That is, there is a liberal usage of excerpted quotations to illustrate the posture of the *Moscow News* (and the other papers) regarding key issues in the Arab-Israeli conflict.

5. *The Straits Times* — 73
   in addition to the quotations and statistical information, there is a discussion of the *Straits Times* reference to the conflict as a "proxy" war.

6. *The Daily Graphic* — Ghana — 91

7. *The Asahi Evening News* — 119

8. *The Times* of London — 145

9. Conclusions — 171
   concluding remarks regarding the research. The remarks summarize the study in terms of each newspaper's position on the key issues of analysis.

   References — 176

Chapter 1

INTRODUCTION

For the last forty years, the Middle East conflict has been in the forefront of international news. Ever since the United Nations voted to partition Palestine in 1947, the plight of Israelis, Palestinians, and the other "actors" in the conflict has been the focus of countless newspaper accounts, television documentaries, books, fact-based novels, made-for-television dramas, and scholarly analyses.

It makes sense that the Middle East has been the subject of such abundant media attention. The conflict is a global one. The international community has been intrigued and interested by the conflict in the Middle East because the international community has been directly and indirectly affected by the conflict during the last forty years. Simply, the "cradle of civilization" might well be the tomb of the same, given the region's strategic economic importance and innate volatility.

The study presented here deals with a specific type of media attention paid to the Middle East conflict. The study focuses on newspaper reactions to the outbreak of the last major war fought in the region. There have been four wars (and innumerable military skirmishes) since Israel achieved statehood. The wars were fought in 1948, 1956, 1967, and 1973. The research here sought to explore the reactions and postures of different world newspapers after the outbreak of the 1973 or Yom Kippur War, so called because its outbreak coincided with the Jewish high holiday, Yom Kippur.

Newspapers do indeed inform and shape opinion. It is valuable, therefore, to examine reports and commentary on specific events to gauge the consistency of these reports and commentary. It is particularly valuable to conduct such analysis when the event itself has worldwide coverage and global impact, as was the case with the Yom Kippur War. Not only did the '73 war have major political implications beyond the Middle East, but the war had tremendous economic implications as well. During the sixty-day period immediately after the outbreak of the fighting, there were oil embargoes implemented to reward those who supported the Arab countries, and punish those who did not. (The study reported here does examine the effect these economic actions had on the positions taken by the newspapers.)

The analysis proved to be illuminating. As will be apparent, there were considerable differences in the nature of the information being disseminated about the fighting, and the events leading up to the fighting. Not only did subjective attitudes vary regarding who was right and who was wrong, but the events themselves were described with dramatic differences. The extent of the variations might be somewhat startling to those unfamiliar with world journalism. Consider the samples cited below.

When the war broke out, the *Times* of London wrote the following as their first editorial words regarding the conflict:

> This time the Arabs started it. Of this there can be no reasonable doubt ("The Fourth Arab-Israeli War," Oct. 8, 1973).

At the same time, the Ghana *Daily Graphic* reacted to the identical event with this commentary:

> As reports indicate, on Saturday [October 6, 1973, the day of the outbreak] several Israeli Air formations attacked Egyptian troops on the Gulf of Suez . . . . At the same time, a number of Israeli navy boats approached the Western coast of the Gulf of Suez . . . Israel has carried on belligerence which is calculated to show off its unmatched military strength in the whole of the Middle East and to humiliate the beleaguered Arabs and taunt them ("War in the Middle East," Oct. 8, 1973).

A Singapore daily held neither the Arabs nor the Israelis responsible for the fighting. The *Straits Times* wrote:

> It has taken a week for a holy war to be shown up as a "proxy war." For despite the tribal, legal, and humanitarian questions involved in the Middle East conflict, the fact is that today, combatants in the fourth Arab-Israeli war are holding on desperately for the "national interests" of the two super powers, the United States and the Soviet Union ("A Proxy War," Oct. 15, 1973).

The *New York Times* took the position that the Arab countries had been the aggressors, but commented that the United Nations was culpable to some extent for its in/activity.

> The armies clash and the bombs fall, civilians perish and the fatuous statesmen on the East River rattle through the corridors asking each other which side would benefit more from a truce ("War or Diplomacy," Oct. 18, 1973).

The *Moscow News* staunchly defended the Arab countries and condemned the Israelis. The *News* wrote:

> In recent days, Israel had established considerable armed forces on the cease fire lines with Syria and, having thereby heated up the situation to the limit, unleashed military operations ("Statement by the Soviet Government," Oct. 20, 1973).

> They [Israel] bear full responsibility for the blood again being spilt in the Middle East ("Firm Support," Oct. 20, 1973).

The *Asahi Evening News*, while indicating that the Arab countries had started the war, were somewhat non-committal.

> It is not clear as to exactly who set the tinder ablaze on Saturday ("Arab-Israeli Conflict," Oct. 9, 1973).

As indicated, the examination of the newspapers reflected considerable diversity. This book provides a quantitative and qualitative report of the nature of this diversity.

Chapter 2

METHODOLOGY

Sample for Analysis

Newspaper editorials and articles akin to editorials (defined below) were used as the sample for the study because they provide the best material for investigating and analyzing perceptions and attitudes. They have been used extensively in previous studies that have had similar purposes. Harold Lasswell used editorials in his classic 1941 RADIR study research, and Ithiel De Sola Pool's study of "Prestige" newspapers in 1951 also employed editorials as the sample. (RADIR is an acronym for Revolution and the Development of International Relations.) Editorials are typically written and read with great care and are rich with national attitudes. Therefore, they become a good sample for this type of research.

The editorials examined for this study appeared in six different newspapers over a two-month period beginning when the war began on October 6, 1973, and ending on December 8, 1973.

Selected Newspapers

The newspapers that provided the editorials were selected on the basis of a number of criteria. Each paper represents a particular geographic region. North America, Europe, Asia, Africa, Southeast Asia, and the Far East are all represented. (Countries belonging to OPEC were excluded from consideration.) Each selected newspaper was a publication that was written either *by* or *for* nationals with the intention of conveying a national perspective. Finally, each newspaper selected was an English language paper.

Not all newspapers published in specific countries reflect perspectives or official political views of that nation. Therefore, in picking appropriate newspapers it was important to select papers that indeed reflected *a* national perspective. (Certainly in democratic countries newspapers will not necessarily reflect *the* national perspective, but will reflect *a* perspective.) The *New York Times International*, published and distributed in Paris, and the *Daily Journal*, published in Caracas, are examples of newspapers which do *not* reflect a national perspective. Both papers are owned and operated by foreign interests and are reflective of the perspectives of the controlling interest. One is more likely, for example, to read about the Houston Oilers of the National Football League in the *Daily Journal* than to see articles about athletic teams competing in Venezuela.

The following section briefly describes and identifies each newspaper selected. The description reflects the paper's characteristics at the time of the '73 war.

Daily Graphic (Ghana). The *Daily Graphic* is published in Accra, Ghana. Ghana has one of Africa's strongest press systems and in 1973 the *Daily Graphic* had the largest circulation of the five dailies in Ghana. Although many languages are used in Ghana, English is widely spoken. The *Daily Graphic* is published by nationals and for nationals.

Times of London (Great Britain). The *Times* of London represents a high quality of journalism and enjoys the prestige of one of the finest and most respected newspapers in the world.

Asahi Evening News (Japan). The *Asahi Evening News* is owned by the same company which publishes the *Asahi Shimbun*, one of three leading Japanese dailies. The English-language *Asahi* is the "sister" paper to the *Shimbun* and, although written in English, is published by nationals with the intention of conveying a national perspective.

Straits Times (Singapore). The *Straits Times* is published in Singapore where, although Chinese is the principal language, English and Malay are also official languages. The *Times* is one of the leading newspapers in the Far East and Southeast Asia, and in 1973 was the largest and most influential paper in Malaysia.

Moscow News (USSR). The *Moscow News* is a weekly publication, chiefly for tourists, but it conveys the national perspective of the USSR. All of the Soviet Union's papers are considered a branch of the government, with the purpose of promulgating government philosophy.

New York Times (United States). The *New York Times*, considered one of the best quality dailies in the US, is read by world leaders to assess at least one perspective--typically a more liberal one than other US dailies--on world and domestic issues.

What Constitutes an "Editorial"

"Editorial" can be a nebulous term. In certain papers, such as the New York or London *Times*, the editorials can be identified readily, for they appear in the same place every day, and are on a page headed "Editorial Page." Yet in other papers, editorials are not so easily distinguished. Sometimes articles are editorialized and it is difficult to draw a clear-cut line between editorials and news stories. If the subject of this study was journalistic technique or format, "editorial" as a descriptor would be inadequate. However, since this study deals with content rather than structure, both editorials and editorialized articles have been used for analysis. What constitutes an editorialized article varies from one paper to another. Prior to the presentation of the information for each newspaper, there is a description of the types of articles included in the sample.

Content Analysis

As mentioned previously, there is a quantitative as well as a qualitative dimension to the analysis. The quantitative dimension is facilitated by the usage of content analysis methodology. Content Analysis is an objective and systematic method for analyzing and quantifying media content. It is intended to provide precise and concise descriptions of what the communication says in terms appropriate to the purpose or problems involved. Content Analysis has been used previously to measure national attitudes and perspectives with editorials employed as the sample for the studies.

Categories for Analysis

The following categories related to the Arab-Israeli conflict were examined. After the list there is an explanation of how the analysis is reported and the operational definitions for the categories.

aggression
land legitimacy
imperialism

intransigence
peace seeking
terrorism
peace seeking
culpability
action justification
Zionism issue
super power culpability
oil diplomacy

For each area or category an assessment was made regarding the posture of the newspaper vis a vis the category.

For example, on the basis of the research, 87 percent of all statements made in the *New York Times* concerning aggression indicated that the Arabs were the aggressors in the conflict. Only 13 percent of these statements indicated that the Israelis' behavior was characterized by aggression. On October 8, the *Times* wrote:

> The aggression perpetrated by Egypt and Syria cannot be condoned or justified in any rational calculation of forces ("Peace Shattered," Oct. 8, 1973).

In the *Moscow News*, 100 percent of all statements made regarding aggression indicated that the Israelis were the aggressors. For example:

> Tel Aviv has committed a new grave act of aggression ("Tel Aviv's Recklessness," Oct. 27, 1973).

> Israel has been for several years now, constantly firing up the situation in the Middle East by its reckless aggressive action ("Statement by the Soviet Government," Oct. 20, 1973).

Below are the operational definitions for each category.

Aggression. Aggression is generally defined as an unprovoked attack or warlike act; specifically, the use of armed forces by a state in violation of its international obligations. The aggressor nation in this study refers to the country that started the conflict, and continued to exhibit aggressive behavior.

Land legitimacy. The land in question is the land that Israel was granted by the UN partition as well as the occupied territory. At the time of the research the occupied territory included the land that Israel has subsequently returned to Egypt in accordance with the Camp David peace treaty.

Imperialism. Imperialism is defined as the policy and practice of forming and maintaining an empire by the conquest of other countries and the establishment of colonies or some type of sphere of influence. Imperialism refers here to either Arab or Israeli policy of land annexation for the purposes of state expansion.

Intransigence. Intransigence refers to either Arab or Israeli stubborn resistance to meet and discuss possibilities for peace.

Peace Seeking. The antithesis of intransigence. It refers to Arab or Israeli genuine willingness to seek and negotiate for peace.

Terrorism. Terrorism is characterized by warlike acts directed against non-combatants (i.e. civilians rather than soldiers).

Culpability. Culpability here refers to the country which is generally deserving of blame for the conflict.

Action justification. This refers to the perceived legitimacy of action(s) taken in the conflict.

Zionism issue. This refers to the practicality of the fundamental tenet of Zionism, the belief that Israel is a sovereign state serving as a homeland for its inhabitants and for Jewish people anywhere who choose to emigrate and become its citizens.

Superpower culpability. This category deals with statements attributing responsibility for the conflict to either the Soviet Union, the United States, or other powerful external sources.

Oil diplomacy. This final category deals with the use of oil as a strategic weapon in resolving the conflict.

Tabulation Procedure

Without becoming too technical, the following is a brief explanation of the procedure for quantifying the data using content analysis methodology.

Each time a sentence in the text contained a statement conveying Arab or Israeli Aggression, Terrorism, Intransigence, etc., a tabulation was made in the respective category.

The *New York Times* and *Moscow News* are again used here to illustrate. In the *New York Times* there were forty-four total tabulations in the category of Aggression during the two-month period of investigation, thirty-eight of which indicated Arab Aggression and six Israeli Aggression. Thus, 87 percent of the total tabulations in the *New York Times* indicated Arab aggression.

In the *Moscow News* there were ninety-seven total tabulations made in the category of Aggression, all indicating Israeli Aggression. Therefore, 100 percent of all statements made regarding aggression indicated that the Israelis were the aggressors.

The procedure was simply a matter of tabulating the frequency of relevant statements and drawing conclusions on the basis of the tabulations.

Uniform Method of Reporting Data

The following chapters present the results of the research. A uniform system for reporting the information has been employed, taking the form of four divisions with appropriate subdivisions.

In the first division, an operational definition for the term editorial for the particular paper is provided. In addition, this division contains statistical information regarding editorial and tabulation frequency.

In the second division, there is an analysis of each category. The analysis consists of the presentation and discussion of the tabulation data in terms of the newspapers' perspectives for each separate category. In addition, this division contains the presentation of numerous excerpted quotations reflecting the positions of the newspaper.

The third division contains information relating specifically to the oil category. In this division there is an examination of the tabulations over time to assess the oil actions' effect on the stated perceptions of the paper. Again, excerpted sections of the articles are provided to illustrate the nature of the positions taken by the newspaper.

The fourth division for each newspaper contains a brief statement of summary and a summary table.

Chapter 3

THE NEW YORK TIMES

Part I. Nature of Editorials

Editorials in the *New York Times* will be defined as (1) those articles appearing on the editorial page under the *Times* banner-head and (2) those articles appearing on the "op-ed" page which are written by members of the editorial board. For illustration, articles on the "op-ed" page by James Reston would be included because Mr. Reston is on the editorial board. However, an article by Dr. Robert Dahl, a political scientist from Yale, was excluded because he is not a member of the editorial board, but simply was a contributor on a given day.

During the period under study, sixty-eight editorials were at least peripherally related to issues in the Middle East conflict. The term "editorial" from this point forth in this chapter refers to these sixty-eight articles.

Editorials appeared on forty-six days of the period being examined, representing 75.4 percent of the days of the period. During the first month after the outbreak of the war, there were only three days in which no editorials appeared. On fifteen days there were two editorials, and on three days, three editorials appeared in the *New York Times*.

The newspaper averaged 1.1 editorials per day and the editorials averaged 483 words in length. There were 370 total tabulations made, 173 of which were in categories other than the Oil category. The Oil category will be analyzed separately in Part III of this chapter. Below and throughout Part II, the phrase "total tabulations" will refer to those exclusive of the Oil category.

There was an average of 2.54 tabulations for each article in the *New York Times*, and an average of .005 tabulations per word. The relevance of these last statistics becomes apparent when comparing the tendencies of the six newspapers. (See Table 174.)

11

Part II. Perspectives on the Key Issues

Aggression

The aggression category had the greatest frequency of tabulations among the bipolar categories, with 25.4 percent of all tabulations appearing in the category. Table 1 presents the frequency and percentage of the total tabulations for each category in the study.

Table 1
Frequency and Percentage of Total Tabulations* for Each Category

Category	Israeli No.	Israeli Pct.	Arab No.	Arab Pct.	Total No	Total Pct.
Aggression	6	3.4	38	21.9	44	25.4
Imperialism	0	0	0	0	0	0
Land legitimacy	6	3.4	1	.5	7	3.9
Terrorism	0	0	0	0	0	0
Peace seeking	21	12.1	22	12.7	43	24.8
Illegitimacy	0	0	1	.5	1	.5
Intransigence	12	6.9	17	9.8	29	16.8
Zionism	0	0	0	0	0	0
Action justif.	1	.5	0	0	1	.5
Culpability	0	0	1	.5	1	.5
Superpower Culpability					47	27.1

*There were 173 tabulations.

Table 2 presents the distribution for the Aggression tabulations. As Table 2 indicates, the statements and corresponding tabulations reflect the *New York Times*' perception of the Arabs as aggressors in the conflict. Of all the Aggression tabulations, 86.4 percent were classed as Arab Aggression and only 13.6 percent as Israeli Aggression.

Table 2
Distribution for
Aggression Tabulations

Aggression Tabulations	Israeli	Arab	Total
Number	6	38	44
Percentage	13.6	86.4	100.0
Tabulations per article	.09	.50	.58
Most in any one day	2	6	

Certain statements from the editorials clearly reveal the newspaper's perspectives regarding this category. For example, on October 8, 1973, the *New York Times* wrote, "The aggression perpetrated by Egypt and Syria cannot be condoned or justified in any rational calculations of forces" ("Peace Shattered," Oct. 8, 1973). Again, on October 9, the *Times* wrote:

> By deluding themselves once again into military adventurism as a cure for political frustration, the leaders of Egypt and Syria seem to have succeeded only in placing themselves and their peoples--as well as people in many lands--into great peril. They risk emerging from the conflict they sparked in a posture far worse than before ("Suicidal Course," Oct. 9, 1973).

On October 12, the newspaper characterized the war as the "latest tragic replay of the Arab ambition to exterminate Israel by force of arms" ("Bedlam at Turtle Bay," Oct. 12, 1973). Not all of the statements tabulated as Arab Aggression are as caustic as these. Many times it was simply stated that the Arabs started the war, or the war was termed the result of Arab aggression.

As Table 2 indicates, Israeli Aggression was tabulated six times. However, in five of these six cases, both Arabs and Israelis were labeled as belligerents. By operational definition, "belligerent" is a qualifier for tabulation. The sixth instance was a criticism of Israeli air attacks. There was an average of .50 Arab Aggression tabulations per article, compared with .09 Israeli Aggression tabulations.

Table 3 represents the percentage of articles containing at least one tabulation for each respective category. As Table 3 indicates, Arab Aggression tabulations appeared more frequently in articles than did tabulations in any other bipolar category. Of the sixty-eight articles, 25.0 percent contained at least one tabulation for Arab aggression and 5.8 percent of the articles contained at least one tabulation for Israeli aggression. It is clear that the *New York Times* perceived the Arabs as the aggressor and that they viewed aggression as a relatively major focus of contention.

Table 3
Frequency and Percentage of
Editorials Containing at Least One
Tabulation for Each Category[a]

Category	Israeli No[b]	Pct[c]	Arab No.	Pct.	Total No	Pct.
Aggression	4	5.8	17	25.0	17	25.0
Imperialism	0	0	0	0	0	0
Land legitimacy	4	5.8	1	1.4	4	5.8
Terrorism	0	0	0	0	0	0
Peace seeking	9	13.2	12	17.6	14	20.6
Illegitimacy	0	0	1	1.4	1	1.4
Intransigence	11	16.1	11	16.1	15	22.1
Zionism	0	0	0	0	0	0
Action Justif.	1	1.4	0	0	1	1.4
Culpability	0	0	1	1.4	1	1.4
Superpower Culp.					21	30.8

[a]This chart would read, for example, re Israeli aggression: four editorials or 5.8 percent of all the editorials contained at least one tabulation for Israeli aggression.

[b]Number of editorials with at least one tabulation.

[c]Percentage of total editorials with at least one tabulation. There were 68 total editorials.

Land Legitimacy

Seven tabulations representing 3.9 percent of the total tabulations were in the Land Legitimacy category. As can be seen in Table 4, the category had a relatively low frequency of tabulations and almost all were in the area of Israeli land legitimacy.

References to Israeli Land Legitimacy did not, however, include the occupied territories but only Israel's "right to exist as a sovereign state" ("Diplomatic Openings," Oct. 17, 1973). Although the *Times* did not sanction land legitimacy rights to the occupied territories, it did imply that it would be wise for Israel to hold on to the territories until a genuine peace was secured. For example, the *Times* writes, "Israel could hardly be expected now, any more than for six years past, to withdraw from the Sinai peninsula before any bargain is struck" (". . . in the Balance," Oct. 19, 1973). This does not affirm eternal rights to the occupied territories, and the newspaper at no time asserts such a claim.

The single Arab Land Legitimacy tabulation corresponds to a statement made concerning the necessity for considering Palestinians' "legitimate rights" when negotiating for peace. The *Times*, however, says that these "legitimate rights" must not be defined as the "option of reclaiming, in what is now the State of Israel, their family homes and properties from before 1948." The newspaper suggests that these legitimate rights could be defined "as the refugees' right to compensation for former properties and the establishment of some kind of 'national home' in the territories now occupied by Israel" (". . . in the Balance," Oct. 19, 1973). This clearly implies the absence of Israeli sovereignty over the occupied territory, but it is the only mention of Palestinian land rights in all of the sixty-eight editorials.

In light of the fact that Land Legitimacy represents only 3.9 percent of the total tabulations, it can be stated generally that the *New York Times* did not consider the question of Land Legitimacy to be an issue worthy of extensive editorial comment.

Table 4
Distribution for Land Legitimacy Tabulations

Land Legitimacy Tabulations	Israeli	Arab	Total
Number	6	1	7
Percentage	85.7	14.3	100.0
Tabulations per article	.08	.01	.09
Most in any one day	2	1	

Peace Seeking

Of all the tabulations for the *New York Times,* 24.8 percent were in the category of Peace Seeking. The category had one fewer tabulation than Aggression (which ranked first among the bipolar areas).

Table 5 illustrates the *Times'* position that both the Arab countries and Israel were making equal efforts toward achieving peace. About half (51.2 percent) of the tabulations were Arab Peace Seeking and half Israeli Peace Seeking (48.8 percent).

Table 5
Distribution for Peace Seeking Tabulations

Peace Seeking Tabulations	Israeli	Arab	Total
Number	21	22	43
Percentage	48.8	51.2	100.0
Tabulations per article	.30	.32	.62
Most in any one day	4	4	

Although the frequency of tabulation was approximately the same, the following quotations show how the presentation of the facts clearly indicates the newspaper's predilections. The first three are consecutive sentences from "Diplomatic Openings" (Oct. 17, 1973). The fourth is from "Diplomacy Triumphant," which appeared on November 12.

1. President Sadat's offer yesterday to accept a ceasefire and to attend a peace conference at the United Nations was qualified with conditions that Israel will clearly not accept.

2. Nevertheless, this first specific indication from the Arab sides of a readiness to halt the fighting which the Egyptians and Syrians began comes in the wake of recent emphasis by Government spokesmen in Cairo on some positive aspects of Egyptian policy, notably assurance that Egypt has no designs on Israel and recognizes her right to exist as a sovereign state.

3. The Sadat proposal for a peace conference suggests the possibility that the Egyptians, having regained their "honor" by moving across the Suez Canal into the Sinai, may be prepared at last to accept face to face talks with the Israelis in some international context ("Diplomatic Openings," Oct. 17, 1973).

4. Mr. Sadat is eagerly pressing for a peace conference as if he had been packed and ready to go all along ("Diplomacy Triumphant," Nov. 12, 1973).

In each of the above quotations the content was appropriately tabulated as Arab Peace Seeking, yet each also includes some type of deprecating remark about the Arab position. In the first quotation, it is implied that Sadat makes a pretense of seeking peace with unrealistic demands for Israel. In the second, although the *Times* allows that there is something positive about Sadat's gesture, it mentions that this is "the first specific indication of a readiness to halt the fighting" and reminds the reader that this is "fighting which the Egyptians and Syrians began." The phrase "at last" in the third quotation, as well as the ironic comment in the fourth, illustrates the *Times'* opinion that, previously, the Arab nations had not sought peace and should have.

A comparison of these Arab Peace Seeking tabulations with some statements coded as Israeli Peace Seeking shows further the newspaper's perspective.

1. Although reports from Israel indicate a hardening of Israeli attitudes on the key issues of returning Arab territories occupied in the six day war of 1967, as well as profound new skepticism about Arab intentions, Premier Golda Meir continues to stress her interest in a cease fire and in peace talks ("Diplomatic Openings," Oct. 17, 1973).

2. Now it is the Israelis, champions of peace negotiations from the start, who seem apprehensive as the path to the conference room is marked out ("Diplomacy Triumphant," Nov. 12, 1973).

3. After years of pressing for peace talks with the Arabs, Israeli diplomats are now in the embarrassing position of having to plead for just a little delay . . ." ("After the New Year," Nov. 28, 1973).

The *Times* editorial board clearly holds the opinion that Israel had been interested in peace earlier than the Arabs. Descriptive phrases are used to reinforce this opinion: Whereas the Arabs "may be prepared at last to accept face to face talks," Israel has been for years "pressing for peace talks." Whereas this is the Arabs' "first specific indication" of peace readiness, the Israelis have been "champions of peace negotiations from the start." Also, sentence structure is used to shift the emphasis. The first Arab Peace Seeking statement quoted above and the first Israeli Peace Seeking statement are from the same editorial of October 17, "Diplomatic Openings." A close comparison of the two is revealing:

Israeli Peace Seeking

Although reports from Israel indicate a hardening of Israeli attitudes on the

Arab Peace Seeking

President Sadat's offer yesterday to accept a ceasefire and to attend a

key issues of returning Arab territories occupied in the six day war of 1967, as well as profound new skepticism about Arab intentions, Premier Golda Meir continues to stress her interests in a ceasefire and in peace talks.

peace conference at the UN was qualified with conditions that Israel will clearly not accept.

Consider the following slight changes in sentence format (italicized words exchanged):

Golda Meir continues to stress her interest in a ceasefire and in peace talks *despite* reports from Israel indicating a hardening of Israeli attitudes on the key issues of returning Arab territories occupied in the six day war of 1967 as well as profound new skepticism about Arab intentions.

Although qualified with conditions that Israel will clearly not accept, President Sadat offered yesterday to accept a ceasefire and to attend a peace conference.

The reversal in clause order and the exchange of the words "although" and "despite" results in a major shift in emphasis. In the original quotation, Golda Meir is depicted as ingenuously striving for peace despite certain obstacles, whereas Sadat appears to advocate peace with unrealistic, relatively intransigent suggestions for attaining it. In the revision, Meir's peace efforts seem more unrealistic and Sadat's initiatives more sincere and less intransigent.

Not all of the statements tabulated as Arab Peace Seeking have modifiers which attenuate their meaning. On October 18, speaking of Sadat, the *Times* writes, "He seems fully prepared to send his representatives to the same bargaining table at which delegates from Israel sit" ("The Oil Gambit," Oct. 18, 1973). Again on November 9, referring to both parties, the *Times* remarks:

> The signals emanating from the Middle East in the wake of Secretary Kissinger's swift passage all point to the imminence of an important compromise, of decisions now made in Cairo and Jerusalem to turn away from military confrontation that threaten the peace

of the world and to enter a political dialogue to achieve the settlement that has eluded warring Arabs and Israelis for so long ("Threshold of Peace," Nov. 9, 1973).

There was an average of .30 Israeli Peace Seeking tabulations per article and .32 Arab Peace Seeking tabulations per article. Of the articles, 13.2 percent contained at least one tabulation for Israeli Peace Seeking and 17.6 percent contained at least one tabulation for Arab Peace Seeking.

Intransigence

Intransigence had the third greatest frequency of tabulations among the bipolar areas, with 16.8 percent. Table 6 presents the distribution, showing only a slight difference in frequency of tabulations for Arab and Israeli Intransigence (58.6 and 41.1 percent, respectively). Again, however, there was a difference in the type of statement tabulated: the Arabs were depicted as stubborn and aloof, while the Israelis were described as justifiably reluctant to deal with the Arabs. For example:

> President Sadat's boastful belligerency and harsh rejection of direct peace talks with Israel at a press conference yesterday were in unfortunate contrast to the diplomatic initiative that was pursued concurrently with apparently serious and constructed purpose, by his new foreign minister in Washington ("Time to Talk," Nov. 1, 1973).

> After years of adamant aloofness, President Hafez Assad has shown marked interest lately in having Syria represent in any Arab peace conference (". . . and Next Syria," Nov. 16, 1973).

In contrast, Israeli intransigence seemed often to be condoned. On October 10, the *Times* writes:

> In the wake of the Arab aggression on Yom Kippur, every additional day of fighting, every fresh Israeli casualty increases Israel's reluctance to yield occupied territory which might serve as a buffer against any future

surprise attack by neighbors unwilling to concede its right to survive ("From Bad to Worse," Oct. 10, 1973).

Table 6
Distribution for
Intransigence Tabulations

Intransigence	Israeli	Arab	Total
Number	12	27	29
Percentage	41.4	58.6	100.0
Tabulations per article	.18	.25	.43
Most in one day	2	4	

A paragraph from the October 21 editorial, "Third Week of Death," is indicative of the different manner in which the *Times* referred to Israeli and Arab intransigence. The first sentence of the quote below was tabulated as Israeli, and the second as Arab, Intransigence:

> [1] The Israelis, *mourning* their dead and fighting to overcome the major disadvantage arising from their willingness to wait until the Arabs struck the first blow, seem hardly in a mood before negotiations even begin, to give up the advantages that possession of the Sinai desert and the Golan Heights provided when the Arabs attacked. [2] And the Arabs, still *intoxicated* by their early triumphs and hopeful that oil blackmail may yet work, give scant evidence of wanting a meaningful compromise--one with any chance of Israeli acceptance ("Third Week of Death," Oct. 21, 1973; italics mine).

Clearly, there is a difference. Israel is "not in the mood" to give up the Sinai because they are "mourning their dead and fighting to overcome a major disadvantage." The Arabs give "scant evidence of wanting a meaningful compromise" because they are "intoxicated by their early triumphs" and are relying upon "oil blackmail."

There was an average of .18 tabulations for Arab Intransigence per article, and .25 tabulations for Arab Intransigence per article. Tabulations for Israeli Intransigence appeared in the same number of editorials. Of the editorials, 16.0 percent in each subcategory had at least one tabulation for Intransigence.

Superpower/International Culpability

The Superpower/International Culpability category had the greatest frequency of tabulation of all the categories. Of the statements tabulated, 27.2 percent attributed some degree of guilt to external parties. A factor to be considered, however, is that the category was not a bipolar one and could have drawn tabulations directed at either nations or international agencies. Yet it is significant that although ostensibly the war involved the Arabs and the Israelis, the *Times* perceived at least certain areas of the tension as being exacerbated by international influence. Table 7 presents the tabulations for this category.

Table 7
Superpower/International Culpability Tabulations*

Superpower/ Internat'l Culp. Tabulations	
Number	47
Percentage of total Tabulations	27.2
per article	.69
Most in any one day	10

*There were 173 total tabulations.

Basically, there were three international parties to which guilt was attributed for some part of the conflict. Most of the tabulations concerned the roles of either the United Nations, the USSR, or the superpowers as a group.

The preponderance of the Culpability statements referred to guilt attributed to the lack of genuine effort to secure peace. This was certainly true of the statements regarding the United Nations. On October 18, for example, the *Times* writes:

> The armies clash and the bombs fall, civilians perish and the fatuous statesmen on the East River rattle through the corridors asking each other which side would benefit more from a truce ("War or Diplomacy," Oct. 10, 1973).

Again, on October 12:

> Secretary General Waldheim's sober appeal for UN action to stop the fighting and press for real peace in the Middle East has as much chance of being heard as a whisper in Bedlam. Nobody is listening ("Bedlam at Turtle Bay," Oct. 12, 1973).

Similarly, the superpowers as a group are admonished for their failure to expedite peace.

> The major nations have agreed to the principle that they have a special responsibility to keep the peace and to work together to prevent others from making war, but in the present crisis between Israel and the Arab states, they have not composed the problem but actually made it worse ("The Hidden Crisis," Oct. 10, 1973).

> Washington and Moscow must devise new ways to use their power and influence, probably through the UN, to mitigate rather than exacerbate Arab and Israeli fears and suspicions and to guarantee the peace they are belatedly trying to promote ("Beyond Ceasefire," Oct. 23, 1973).

The *Times* additionally implies that the major powers are involved strategically, if not militarily:

> Although the Middle East ceasefire is still far from secure, military experts in Washington and Tel Aviv, Moscow and Cairo, already are

> studying the lessons of the fourth Arab-Israeli war and planning the revision in tactics and armaments that might change their fortune in a possible fifth round ("The Proving Ground," Nov. 3, 1973).

In the same article:

> It is obvious that the Middle East has become, like Spain in the 1930's, an important proving ground for the weapons systems of the major powers ("The Proving Ground," Nov. 3, 1973).

Although the major powers and the United Nations are censured by the *Times,* the most vitriolic statements issued in this category were reserved for Moscow. Indeed, despite mention of the mutual culpability of the superpowers, the *Times* castigates Moscow not only for exacerbating the conflict but also for not joining Washington in its efforts for peace. In light of the disparaging statements regarding Washington-style diplomacy quoted above, this is quite enigmatic; yet there are numerous examples of this criticism. The following statements are typical:

> Washington appears to be doing its share in this endeavor [seeking peace], but thus far, Moscow is dragging its feet ("Suicidal Course," Oct. 19, 1973).

> The United States has been using all its influence to bring the fighting to an immediate end--an endeavor in which it should have been joined from the first by Moscow. Instead, the Russians are carrying on their mammoth resupply operation in the face of incontrovertible evidence that the two Arab nations were the initiators of the bloodshed ("Irresponsibility," Oct. 11, 1973).

> The United States is clearly eager to cooperate in containing and ending the conflict. No similar will is evident in the Soviet Union ("Flashpoint," Oct. 16, 1973).

> It was not until Israel had changed the whole military perspective of the struggle . . . that

Moscow suddenly became interested in a ceasefire. It seems a fair guess that if Egypt and Syria had continued to enjoy the military upper hand which their initial surprise attack gave them, Moscow would still be uninterested in any ceasefire proposals ("In Place of Euphoria," Oct. 30, 1973).

It is becoming increasingly clear that the Kremlin is doing much to inflame the Middle East conflict and expand the scope of hostility by large scale aid and incitation of Arabs ("The Hidden Crisis," Oct. 10, 1973).

As Table 8 indicates, most of the tabulations (85.2 percent) cited Moscow, either alone or with another country, as being culpable for some portion of the conflict; well over half cited Moscow alone (59.6 percent). In one editorial, "Irresponsibility," ten statements were made indicting Russia. This was the largest number of tabulations in any one category in any of the articles.

Regarding United States involvement, the editorial position of the *Times* is not so clear. At times the paper praises Washington and at times it does not. However, while there were twenty-eight statements singling out the Soviet Union as a guilty party, no statement charged the United States individually. It seems safe to conclude that the *Times* felt that the United States was not devoid of guilt but relatively guilt-free when compared to the other superpower. Almost a third (30.9 percent) of the sixty-eight articles had tabulations in the Culpability category, and an average of .69 tabulations per article.

Table 8
Distribution of Superpower/
International Culpability Tabulations

Superpower/ Internat'l Culp. Tabulations	UN	Moscow/ Peking	Major Power	Moscow	Total
Number	7	2	10	28	47
Percentage	14.8	4.3	21.3	59.6	100.0
Tabs per article	.10	.05	.14	.41	.70

*Illegitimacy - Action Justification -
Culpability*

There was only one tabulation in each of the three areas of Illegitimacy, Action Justification and Culpability. In each of these three cases, the tabulation was a pro-Israeli one.

*Imperialism, Terrorism
and Zionism*

There were no tabulations in any of the sixty-eight articles for either Arab or Israeli Terrorism, Imperialism, or the practicality or impracticality of Zionism.

Part III. The Impact of Oil

The Oil category had the greatest frequency of tabulation of all, more than four times the tabulations of the next highest category. (As mentioned previously, discussion in this category will be based on the complete total of 370 tabulations.) The Oil category alone had twenty-four more tabulations than all other categories combined (see Table 9), so it is clear that oil was a pervasive concern for the *New York Times*. However, the relatively high tabulation percentage is in part due to the fact that any time oil or energy appeared within the context of an article dealing with even the most peripheral aspects of the conflict, the symbol was tabulated in the Oil category. Given this difference in scope, it is apparent that too many comparisons with the other categories would be unproductive. Yet the high tabulation frequency does reflect the reality that it was an issue of great concern to the paper. Almost half of the articles studied (42.7 percent) had at least one tabulation in the Oil category.

Table 9
Frequency and Percentage of
Total Tabulations for Each Category
Including Oil*

Category	Number	Percentage of Total
Oil	197	53.2
Aggression	44	11.9
Imperialism	0	0
Land legitimacy	7	1.9
Terrorism	0	0
Peace seeking	43	11.6
Illegitimacy	1	.3
Intransigence	29	7.8
Zionism	0	0
Action Justification	1	.3
Culpability	1	.3
Superpower Culpability	47	12.7

*N = 370.

There were 2.89 tabulations in Oil per article. Eight articles had more than ten tabulations for Oil, and one had over twenty. Some articles, of course, had oil as the major focus, so that ten tabulations, considering the extent of qualification criteria, would not be surprising.

Tables 10 through 19 examine the categories in relation to three time periods: (1) October 6 - 17, 1973; (2) October 18 - November 5, and (3) November 6 - December 8. These periods correspond to the Arab oil actions affecting nations supporting Israel. There were two such embargoes. The first, on October 17, was directed at the United States. The second embargo, on November 5, 1973, affected not only the U.S. but other Israeli sympathizers. Table 10 presents a distribution for the Oil category over time.

Table 10
Oil Tabulations Distributed Over Three Time Periods

Oil Tabulations	Oct. 6 - Oct. 17	Oct. 18 - Nov. 5	Nov. 6 - Dec. 8
Number	29	19	149
Percentage	14.7	9.6	75.6

As might be expected, most of the tabulations (85.2 percent) appeared after the embargo of October 17. It would seem from the data in Table 10 that the *Times* became more concerned with oil as an issue after it had ramifications for countries other than the United States. This does make sense. The effect of the oil action in terms of a possible American capitulation to a pro-Arab policy was negligible. However, a change in the policies of other nations was not that remote. England had come out with a questionable "even-handed" policy which involved granting military aid neither to Israelis or Arabs, despite precedent for sending aid to Israel. Japan was in desperate economic straits and the European Economic Community had issued a statement supporting the Arab countries. There was a concern in the U.S. for the absence of international Israeli support and this is likely why 75.4 percent of the oil tabulations occurred when they did.

Table 11 indicates that the oil embargo had no effect on the number of articles printed during the three periods. As would be expected, as the time from the start of the war increased, the number of articles regarding the conflict decreased. It is significant, however, that 37.9 percent of the articles in the third period dealt primarily with oil. That is, of the twenty-nine articles written in the third period, eleven had no other tabulations except for those in the Oil category.

Table 11
Editorial Frequency
Over Three Time Periods

Editorials (N = 68)	Oct. 6 - Oct. 17	Oct. 18 - Nov. 5	Nov. 6 - Dec. 8
Number of days	11	20	32
Number of editorials	16	23	29
Editorials/day	1.45	1.15	.91
Percentage of total editorials	23.5	29.4	47.1

The *Times* editorial policy exhibited little evidence of being affected by the oil embargo. The *Times* writes on November 23, 1973:

> Secretary of State Kissinger has properly warned that this country's Middle East policies stand on their own merits and will not be altered under pressure of an oil embargo ("The Arab Oil Threat," Nov. 23, 1973).

The fact that the *Times* considered this a "proper warning" is substantiated by the analysis of the data over time. The *Times* remained pro-Israeli throughout the period of examination. The only variation that might have been a function of economic action appeared in the frequency of certain statements in some categories. A review of each bipolar category over the three time periods corresponding to the oil actions supports this lack of vacillation and the periodic frequency differences.

Aggression Over Time

Table 12 presents the data on Aggression tabulations in the three time periods. Arab Aggression statements decreased with time whereas statements regarding Israeli Aggression remained the same for the first two periods before decreasing for the third. Little can be concluded from these data. Since aggression is defined, in part, as the starting of the conflict, it stands to reason that a greater percentage of Aggression statements would be made in the initial period. There was no evidence of a reversal in position on the part of the *Times*.

Table 12
Aggression Tabulations
Distributed over the
Three Time Periods

Category	Oct. 6-17 No[a]	Oct. 6-17 Pct[b]	Oct. 18 - Nov. 5 No.	Oct. 18 - Nov. 5 Pct.	Nov. 6 - Dec. 8 No	Nov. 6 - Dec. 8 Pct.
Israeli	3	50.0	3	50.0	0	0.0
Arab	22	57.9	13	34.2	3	7.9
Total	25	56.8	16	36.4	3	6.8

[a]Number of tabulations.
[b]Percentage of tabulations in respective category.

Table 13 presents data concerning the frequency with which tabulations on Aggression appeared in articles during each time period. On 56.2 percent of the days in the first period, there was at least one tabulation regarding Arab Aggression, falling to 21.7 percent in the second and 10.3 percent in the third period. As discussed earlier, however, this does not suggest any shift in position due to economic factors.

Table 13
Articles in Which at Least One
Aggression Tabulation Occurs

Category	Oct. 6-17 No[a]	Oct. 6-17 Pct[b]	Oct. 18 - Nov. 5 No.	Oct. 18 - Nov. 5 Pct.	Nov. 6 - Dec. 8 No	Nov. 6 - Dec. 8 Pct.
Israeli	2	12.5	2	8.7	0	0.0
Arab	9	56.2	5	21.7	3	10.3
Total	9	56.2	5	21.7	3	10.3

[a]Number of articles with at least one Aggression tabulation.
[b]Percentage of articles with at least one tabulation.

Land Legitimacy Over Time

As Tables 14 and 15 indicate, the *Times* did not alter its perspective on land legitimacy, nor did it increase its interest in the category. Although there were Israeli Land Legitimacy tabulations in only 4.3 percent of the articles in the second period as compared with 12.5 percent in the first, this represents a difference of only one article, albeit over a slightly longer period of time.

Table 14
Land Legitimacy Tabulations
Distributed over the Time Periods

Category	Oct. 6-17 No[a]	Oct. 6-17 Pct[b]	Oct. 18 - Nov. 5 No.	Oct. 18 - Nov. 5 Pct.	Nov. 6 - Dec. 8 No	Nov. 6 - Dec. 8 Pct.
Israeli	2	33.3	2	33.3	2	33.3
Arab	0	0.0	1	100.0	0	0.0
Total	2	28.6	3	42.9	2	28.6

[a]Number of tabulations.
[b]Percentage of tabulations in respective category.

Table 15
**Articles in Which at Least One
Land Legitimacy Tabulation Occurs
Over Three Time Periods**

Category	Oct. 6-17		Oct. 18 - Nov. 5		Nov. 6 - Dec. 8	
	No[a]	Pct[b]	No.	Pct.	No	Pct.
Israeli	2	12.5	1	4.3	1	3.4
Arab	0	0.0	1	4.3	0	0.0
Total	2	12.5	2	8.7	1	3.4

[a]Number of articles with at least one Land Legitimacy tabulation.
[b]Percentage of articles with at least one tabulation.

Peace Seeking Over Time

Table 16 indicates that tabulations for Peace Seeking increased over time consistently for both parties in the conflict. After the first oil action, more comments were made regarding efforts to achieve peace. Additionally, as Table 17 indicates, whereas only 6.2 percent of the articles in the first period had Peace Seeking tabulations, 26.1 percent in the second and 24.1 percent of the articles in the third period had Peace Seeking tabulations. Taken by itself, this might indicate a greater concern for peace once the ramifications of the conflict appeared to have national and international implications. The data in the related area of Intransigence support this supposition.

Table 16
Peace Seeking Tabulations
Distributed over the
Three Time Periods

Category	Oct. 6-17 No[a]	Pct[b]	Oct. 18 - Nov. 5 No.	Pct.	Nov. 6 - Dec. 8 No	Pct.
Israeli	1	4.8	7	33.3	13	61.9
Arab	3	13.6	7	33.3	12	54.5
Total	3	7.0	15	34.9	25	58.1

[a]Number of tabulations.
[b]Percentage of tabulations in respective category.

Table 17
Articles in Which at Least One
Peace Seeking Tabulation Occurs
Over Three Time Periods

Category	Oct. 6-17 No[a]	Pct[b]	Oct. 18 - Nov. 5 No.	Pct.	Nov. 6 - Dec. 8 No	Pct.
Israeli	1	6.2	4	17.4	5	17.2
Arab	1	6.2	5	21.7	6	20.7
Total	1	6.2	6	26.1	7	24.1

[a]Number of articles with at least one Peace Seeking tabulation.
[b]Percentage of articles with at least one tabulation.

Intransigence Over Time

Table 18 indicates that the *Times* increased its statements tabulated as Israeli Intransigence by 17 percent in each of the last two periods. There were no statements tabulated as Arab Intransigence in the first period, seven in the second and ten in the third. The fact that 93 percent of all the tabulations in this area appeared after the first embargo affecting the United States suggests that, as it became apparent that peace in the Mideast would mean a reduction of problems involving energy, the *New York Times* became more concerned with which party was more unyielding regarding efforts for peace. It is also possible that these results are a simple function of the fact that the longer the conflict dragged on, the more concerned the *Times* became with the intransigence of either party. The *Times* did not reconsider its pro-Israeli stand because of oil pressure, but national and international considerations may have moved it toward a greater concern for peace. In the related areas of Peace Seeking and Intransigence, sixty-seven of the seventy-two tabulations (93.1 percent) appeared after October 17. As Table 19 indicates, 86.7 percent of the articles which contained Intransigence tabulations appeared after October 17. The combination of the related categories reveals that 89.7 percent of articles which contained Intransigence and Peace Seeking tabulations appeared after October 17, 1973.

Table 18
Intransigence Tabulations
Distributed over the
Three Time Periods

Category	Oct. 6-17 No[a]	Pct[b]	Oct. 18 - Nov. 5 No.	Pct.	Nov. 6 - Dec. 8 No	Pct.
Israeli	2	16.7	4	33.3	6	50.0
Arab	0	0.0	7	41.2	10	58.8
Total	2	6.9	11	37.9	16	55.2

[a]Number of tabulations.
[b]Percentage of tabulations in respective category.

Table 19
Articles in Which at Least One Intransigence Tabulation Occurs Over Three Time Periods

Category	Oct. 6-17 No[a]	Pct[b]	Oct. 18 - Nov. 5 No.	Pct.	Nov. 6 - Dec. 8 No	Pct.
Israeli	2	12.5	4	17.4	5	17.2
Arab	0	0.0	6	26.1	5	17.2
Total	2	12.5	7	30.4	6	20.7

[a]Number of articles with at least one Intransigence tabulation.
[b]Percentage of articles with at least one tabulation.

The above data show that there were no substantive shifts in perspective in the *New York Times* as a result of the oil embargoes. Far from allowing the embargoes to influence its position, the *Times* was unequivocally negative toward them throughout the period in question. The negative attitude often manifested itself in veiled (or not veiled) threatening messages. Before the enactment of the first embargo, the *Times* attempted to discourage a possible Arab oil action:

> The Arabs would be wise to recognize that nations which did not bow to Stalin's threats are not likely to surrender to theirs. History makes it excessively plain that capitulation to blackmail merely invites its endless extension ("Oil Blackmail," Oct. 17, 1973).

After the first embargo, the *Times* wrote:

> ... the United States cannot be blackmailed into abandoning its fundamental commitment to Israel's survival and security ("The Oil Gambit," Oct. 18, 1973).

The *Times* became more hostile after the enactment of the second embargo, which was extended to affect all nations not sympathetic to the Arab cause. Warning other nations not to succumb to external pressures, the *Times* drew a severe analogy:

> The nations of Europe, Japan and the United States must face up to the choice that now confronts them: whether each nation should seek special deals with the Arabs or whether they will work together for their collective security and well being. The first course, however tempting it may seem to some countries in the short run, cannot work for long, any more than did appeasement at Munich ("The Oil Weapon," Nov. 6, 1973).

A further warning appeared later:

> Their oil in fact, is a wasting asset; the current crisis is compelling action to develop new energy sources that in any case would have to be taken by the end of the century...
>
> If the Arabs overplay their hand, they are bound to solidify the West against them and ultimately bring on retaliation...
>
> The oil embargo they have launched is an act of both political and economic warfare accompanied as it seems to be, by all sorts of inflammatory and extravagant threats ... If they entertain any illusions on this score, the Arabs must soon be disabused of the notion that they can go on waging war with impunity ("The Arab Oil Threat," Nov. 23, 1973).

A check of the titles of the editorials relating to oil is enough to get a clear picture of the *Times'* perspective: "Oily Diplomacy," "Oil Blackmail," "The Oil Gambit," "The Oil Weapon," "The Arab Oil Threat," and "Dangerous Oils."

Briefly, oil permeated the *Times'* consciousness to the extent that 42.7 percent of the sixty-eight articles examined contained at least one mention of oil. Their opinion of the embargo was that it was inappropriate, equivalent to blackmail, and would not be surrendered to. The effect of the embargo on their positions regarding the other categories was negligible.

Part IV. Summary: *The New York Times*

Table 20 presents the distribution of the overall tabulations, revealing that the *Times* was generally pro-Israel in its editorial policy.

Table 20
Overall Tabulations

Category	Pro-Israeli	Pro-Arab
Aggression	38	6
Imperialism	0	0
Land legitimacy	6	1
Terrorism	0	0
Peace seeking	21	22
Illegitimacy	1	0
Intransigence	17	12
Zionism	0	0
Action justif.	1	0
Culpability	1	0
Total	85	41
Percentage of Total	67.4	32.5

*N = 173.

The statements defined as advocating a pro-Israeli position constituted about two-thirds of the total tabulations, far outweighing those defined as pro-Arab. The *New York Times* editorial position can be summarized as follows:

1. The Arabs were the aggressors.
2. Israel has the right to exist as a state.
    a. Israel has the right to possess the territories, as the territories at this time (1973) provide security.
    b. Israel does not have eternal land rights to the territories.
    c. The Palestinians have rights to land, but not to the pre-1967 State of Israel.
3. The Arabs and Israelis both took initiatives to secure peace.
    a. Israel had always made peace initiatives.

  b. The Arabs had not always made peace initiatives.
4. Both Arabs and Israelis are intransigent.
  a. Israelis have some justification for being intransigent.
  b. The Arabs have little justification for being intransigent.
5. The US, the UN, and the USSR were guilty of actions or non-actions which exacerbated the conflict.
  a. The Soviet Union is particularly culpable for not using its influence as a superpower to create peace opportunities.
  c. The United States and the Soviet Union were at least peripherally involved militarily.
6. Oil diplomacy is inappropriate and equivalent to blackmail.
7. Neither terrorism, imperialism, or Zionism are issues of sufficient magnitude in this conflict to warrant extensive editorial comment.
8. The *Times* did not alter its communications as a result of the Arab oil action.

Chapter 4

THE MOSCOW NEWS

Part I. Nature of Editorials

The purpose of the Soviet press is to promulgate the philosophy of the government of the USSR. The *Moscow News*, consistent with that philosophy, reports and editorializes in the same columns. The *News* does not have an editorial page or section as such; rather, each article gives the opinions of the editors or publishers, which in turn are essentially the views of the government. Therefore, for the purposes of this study, editorials in the *Moscow News* are defined as any articles dealing with the Middle East conflict. Nineteen such articles were found in the *News* in the period being examined. Henceforth the word editorials will refer to those nineteen articles.

There were ten editions of the *News* during the examination period. As noted earlier, the *News* is a weekly publication, and like many other weeklies, it postdates its editions. The issue dated October 13-20, 1973, for example, was written previous to that date. According to the U.S. Postal Service, mail takes an average of one week to travel from Moscow to New York. The October 13-20 issue, which was received by the Buffalo and Erie County Public Library on October 11, was probably written by October 6 at the latest. Using this method of determining dates, issues dating from October 20-27 (received at the library October 14) through December 22-29 (received December 17) were the ones examined.

All of the issues contained at least one editorial on the Middle East. One issue contained five editorials and another four. There was an average of 1.9 editorials per issue. The *News* averaged 617.9 words per editorial with a total of approximately 11,740 words in articles dealing with the Middle East conflict. In the nineteen articles, there were 348 tabulations and 333 tabulations exclusive of the Oil category. As before, in the following section, "total" tabulations refers to tabulations exclusive of the Oil category. There was an average of 17.5 tabulations exclusive of those in the Oil category. Again, the Oil category will be discussed separately.

Part II. Perspectives on Key Issues

Aggression

The Aggression category had the highest frequency of tabulations, with 97 of the 333 tabulations (29.1 percent). Table 21 presents the frequency and percentage of the total tabulations for each category in the study. As indicated, the Aggression category had more than twice the tabulation frequency of any one of the other categories.

Table 21
Frequency and Percentage of
Total Tabulations for Each Category*

Category	Israeli No.	Israeli Pct.	Arab No.	Arab Pct.	Total No	Total Pct.
Aggression	97	29.1	0	0.0	97	29.1
Imperialism	28	8.4	0	0.0	28	8.4
Land legitimacy	0	0.0	27	8.1	27	8.1
Terrorism	46	13.8	0	0.0	46	13.8
Peace seeking	2	.6	9	2.7	11	3.3
Illegitimacy	21	6.3	0	0.0	21	6.3
Intransigence	44	13.2	0	0.0	44	13.2
Zionism	0	0.0	4	1.2	4	1.2
Action justif.	0	0.0	18	5.4	18	5.4
Culpability	18	5.4	0	0.0	18	5.4
Superpowers					19	5.7

*Total tabulations = 333.

Table 22 on the following page presents the distribution of the Aggression tabulations. It is clear that the *Moscow News* considered the Israelis the aggressors in the conflict. They unequivocally state, "A battle is raging between the aggressor Israel and the victims of aggression, Egypt and Syria" ("Tel Aviv's Recklessness," Oct. 20, 1973). As Table 22 indicates, 100 percent of the tabulations were in the Israeli column. The *News* repeatedly admonished the Israelis for their purported aggressive behavior. In three editorials more than ten tabulations for

Israeli Aggression were charted ("Statement by the Soviet Government," Oct. 20; "Tel Aviv's Recklessness," Oct. 14; and "Tel Aviv's Recklessness," Oct. 27). There was an average of 5.1 Israeli Aggression tabulations per article.

Table 22
Distribution for
Aggression Tabulations

Aggression Tabulations	Israeli	Arab	Total
Number	97	0	97
Percentage	100.0	0.0	100.0
Tabulations per article	5.1	0	5.1
Most in any one day	12	0	

The following typical examples of statements tabulated in this category reveal the unequivocal nature of the newspaper's posture:

> In recent days, Israel had established considerable armed forces on the cease fire lines with Syria and Egypt, had called up reservists and, having thereby heated up the situation to the limit, unleashed military operations ("Statement by the Soviet Government," Oct. 20, 1973).
>
> As a result of Israel's stubborn continuation of aggression against the Arab countries, military operations have again flared up in the Middle East ("Firm Support," Oct. 20, 1973).
>
> Israel has been for several years now, constantly firing up the situation in the Middle East by its reckless aggressive action ("Statement by the Soviet Government," Oct. 20, 1973).

Tel Aviv has committed a new grave act of aggression ("Tel Aviv's Recklessness," Oct. 27, 1973).

Each of the nineteen articles contained at least one tabulation for Israeli Aggression. Table 23 presents the frequency and percentage of articles in which there was at least one tabulation for each category. As is evident from the chart, Israeli Aggression is the only category with tabulations in every article. It is apparent that the *News* considered aggression an important focus of contention in the conflict.

Table 23
Frequency and Percentage of Editorials Containing at Least One Tabulation for Each Category

Category	Israeli No.[a]	Pct.[b]	Arab No.	Pct.	Total No	Pct.
Aggression	19	100.0	0	0.0	19	100.0
Imperialism	12	63.1	0	0.0	12	63.1
Land legitimacy	0	0.0	17	89.5	17	89.5
Terrorism	9	47.3	0	0.0	9	47.3
Peace seeking	2	10.5	5	26.3	5	26.3
Illegitimacy	13	68.4	0	0.0	13	68.4
Intransigence	17	89.5	0	0.0	17	89.5
Zionism	0	0.0	3	15.0	3	15.0
Action justif.	0	0.0	11	57.8	11	57.8
Culpability	11	57.8	0	0.0	11	57.8
Superpowers					10	52.6

[a]Number of editorials with at least one tabulation. There were 19 total editorials.
[b]Percentage of total editorial with at least one tabulation.

Imperialism

The category of Imperialism accounted for 8.4 percent of the total tabulations, ranking fourth in tabulation frequency. Table 24 presents the distribution, indicating that all tabulations were in the Israeli column.

**Table 24
Distribution for
Imperialism Tabulations**

Imperialism Tabulations	Israeli	Arab	Total
Number	28	0	28
Percentage	100.0	0.0	100.0
Tabulations per article	1.47	0.0	1.47
Most in any one day	4	0	

The *News* felt that Israel's imperialistic tendency toward political expansionism was the root cause of the war. They write:

> It is no secret to anyone that the cause of this situation is the expansionist policy of Israel ("Statement by the Soviet Government," Oct. 20, 1973).
>
> ... the cause of the present situation in the Middle East is the expansionist policies of Israel's ruling circles ("Firm Support," Oct. 20, 1973).
>
> The Israeli aggressors ... seek to keep the Middle East in an explosive state which they need to effect their far reaching expansionist designs ("Firm Support," Oct. 20, 1973).

The statements are typically "condemning the expansionist policy of Israel" or characterizing the Israeli government as "fascinated by its expansionist ambition" ("Statement by the Soviet Government," Oct. 14, 1973). There were 1.47 tabulations for Israeli Imperialism per article. Statements which were tabulated as Israeli Imperialism appeared in twelve of the nineteen articles (63.2 percent).

Land Legitimacy

There were twenty-seven tabulations, representing 8.1 percent of the total, in the area of Land Legitimacy. Table 25 presents the distribution of tabulations, all of which were in the area of Arab Land Legitimacy.

**Table 25
Distribution for
Land Legitimacy Tabulations**

Land Legitimacy Tabulations	Israeli	Arab	Total
Number	0	27	27
Percentage	0.0	100.0	100.0
Tabulations per article	0.0	1.42	1.42
Most in any one day	0	3	

The *News* was adamant regarding the Palestinian right to the "occupied territories." An article in the December 8 issue, for example, reads:

> All Israel-occupied territories must be returned to the Arab States and the lawful rights of the Arab population of Palestine must be restored ("Arab Unity Strengthening," Dec. 8, 1973).

Again, on October 27, they write:

> Israeli troops must be withdrawn from all Arab territories occupied since 1967 and all parties must recognize the legitimate rights of the Arab people of Palestine ("Denouncement and Support," Oct. 27, 1973).

The *News*, however, did not take a clear stand regarding the legitimacy of Israel's statehood. The closest comment to such a sanctioning appeared in a November 10 editorial entitled "The Road to Peace in the Middle East":

> . . . the view recently expressed in the *Washington Post* is worth noting. It *[sic]* wrote that although *Israel had the right to existence,* the recent developments again posed the question of whether Israel had the right to continuously occupy alien territories, provoke the vengeance of the Arabs, and a dragged-out local conflict [sic], and maintain the constant threat of a third world war.
>
> To this reasonable question, the nations of the whole world answer firmly and unequivocally: NO! ("The Road to Peace in the Middle East," Nov. 10, 1973; italics mine).

Although the article itself does not speak in favor of Israel's right to exist, the inclusion and non-refutation of the italicized clause suggest agreement. Had *The News* chosen, it could easily have begun the excerpted passage with the words, "the recent developments." Thus the reader can infer some type of tacit approval or, more likely in light of its overall philosophy, at least acknowledgement of the existence of the State of Israel. No explicit statement was made, however, so a definite philosophy cannot be determined.

Seventeen of the nineteen articles (89.5 percent) had at least one tabulation for Arab Land Legitimacy. The *News* apparently considered the land legitimacy of the Arabs an important area of contention.

Terrorism

Terrorism ranked second among the categories, with forty-six tabulations or 13.8 percent of the total. Table 26 presents the distribution which, as in previous categories, is monodimensional. All forty-six of the tabulations were in the area of Israeli Terrorism.

Table 26
Distribution for
Terrorism Tabulations

Terrorism Tabulations	Israeli	Arab	Total
Number	46	0	46
Percentage	100.0	0.0	100.0
Tabulations per article	2.42	0.0	2.42
Most in any one day	22	0	

The *News* vehemently condemned the alleged Israeli terrorist acts. The newspaper writes:

> . . . the Israeli military are turning lethal weapons against peaceful citizens, against civilian targets and even carry out attacks on the ships and purely civilian institutions of states that take no part in the war ("Tass Statement," Oct. 27, 1973).

> This month's hostilities reached unparalleled intensities with heavy casualties on both sides including the loss of life among the civilian population as a result of the barbaric bombing of peaceful towns and villages in Egypt and Syria ("The War in the Middle East Must End," Nov. 17, 1973).

> Recent events have ripped away the masks from the Israeli chieftains. They are using deadly weapons against civilian and nonmilitary targets. Many towns in Syria and Egypt have been barbariously bombed and many civilians have been killed ("Tel Aviv's Recklessness," Oct. 27, 1973).

> On October 9, Israeli aircraft dropped bombs on the Soviet cultural center situated in one of the districts of Damascus, where there are

no military targets, but only missions of foreign states. There are victims among Soviet and Syrian citizens who were in this building ("Tass Statement," Oct. 27, 1973).

The *News* is consistently vitriolic in their condemnation of the alleged acts of terrorism, with at least one tabulation in nine of the nineteen articles. One of them, "Tass Statement," had twenty-two tabulations.

Peace Seeking

There were eleven tabulations in the area of Peace Seeking, or 3.3 percent of the total tabulations. The only category which had fewer was the one concerning the practicality of Zionism. Table 27 presents the distribution.

Table 27
Distribution for
Peace Seeking Tabulations

Peace Seeking Tabulations	Israeli	Arab	Total
Number	2	9	11
Percentage	18.2	81.8	100.0
Tabulations per article	.11	.47	.58
Most in any one day	1	3	

This category was the only one among the ten bipolar categories which was indeed two-dimensional. However, tabulations for Arab Peace Seeking (81.8 percent) far outnumbered those for Israeli Peace Seeking (18.2 percent). It was clear that the *News* considered the Arabs to be the party which ingenuously and continually sought peace.

It is well known that the Arab states have shown quite a lot of restraint and readiness to seek a political settlement of the conflict on a just basis ("Statement by the Soviet Government," Oct. 20, 1973).

> Everyone is well aware that the Arab states have displayed utmost restraint and a preparedness to accept a political settlement on a just basis ("Tel Aviv's Recklessness," Oct. 27, 1973).
>
> The Arab people are alien to warmongering ("Just Settlement for the Middle East," Dec. 1, 1973).

Israeli Peace Seeking was mentioned only twice:

> Representatives of the A.R.E. and Israel signed a document concerning the observance of the cease fire agreement ("Undelayed Task," Nov. 24, 1973).
>
> Recently Egypt and Israel began exchanging prisoners in accordance with the bilateral protocol of November 11. The fact in itself is positive ("Just Settlement for the Middle East," Dec. 1, 1973).

In neither case were the Israeli Peace Seeking efforts seen as unilateral. There were no statements regarding any initiatives taken by Israel to secure peace. In fact, the second statement quoted above is immediately followed by this qualifier:

> However, Israel is stubbornly refusing to observe other provisions of the protocol on a ceasefire and the withdrawal of troops to the positions of October 22 ("Just Settlement for the Middle East," Dec. 1, 1973).

Five of the nineteen articles (26.3 percent) had Arab Peace Seeking tabulations, and two (10.5 percent) had Israeli Peace Seeking tabulations.

Illegitimacy

There were 21 tabulations in this category, representing 6.3 percent of the total and ranking the issue sixth in frequency among the categories. Table 28 presents the Illegitimacy distribution, showing all tabulations in the area of Israeli Illegitimacy.

Table 28
Distribution for Illegitimacy Tabulations

Illegitimacy Tabulations	Israeli	Arab	Total
Number	21	0	21
Percentage	100.0	0.0	100.0
Tabulations per article	1.1	0.0	1.1
Most in any one day	5	0	

As would be expected from examining the data in the related area of Land Legitimacy, the *News* felt that Israel's position was not legitimate and called for Israeli withdrawal from territory which did not belong to them. Thirteen of the nineteen articles had tabulations in the area of Land Legitimacy, a frequency of 68.4 percent.

Intransigence

There were forty-four tabulations in this area, again all in the Israeli column, as shown in Table 29. The Intransigence category had the third highest frequency, with 13.2 percent of the total tabulations.

Table 29
Distribution for Intransigence Tabulations

Intransigence Tabulations	Israeli	Arab	Total
Number	44	0	44
Percentage	100.0	0.0	100.0
Tabulations per article	2.3	0.0	2.3
Most in any one day	8	0	

Moscow perceived the Israelis as sabotaging peace efforts intended to resolve the conflict. The following are typical of the repeated statements to this effect in the *News*:

> The efforts of the Arab countries have invariably come up against Tel Aviv's obstructionist position ("Statement by the Soviet Government," Oct. 20, 1973).
>
> Israel has obstructed the efforts to bring about a fair settlement of the Middle East conflict ("Firm Support," Oct. 20, 1973).
>
> Tel Aviv has sabotaged all attempts at a just political settlement in the Middle East ("Tel Aviv's Recklessness," Oct. 27, 1973).
>
> The Israeli aggressors having engineered a new eruption of hostilities in the Middle East crisis, are going out of their way to sabotage the Octover 22nd and 23rd Security Council resolutions . . . ("The Road to Peace in the Middle East," Nov. 10, 1973).
>
> Tel Aviv has in every way obstructed the operation of the UN Task Force ("Undelayed Task," Nov. 24, 1973).

Israel is characterized as "frustrating all the efforts aimed at establishing a just peace" ("Statement by the Soviet Government," Oct. 20, 1973). There were 2.3 tabulations per article in this category. Seventeen of the nineteen articles (89.5 percent) contain tabulations in the category of Israeli Intransigence. This intransigence as indicated by its frequency was considered by the *News* to be a major area of contention.

Zionism

Zionism tabulations were the most infrequent compared to the other categories, with only four in the entire period (1.2 percent of the total). Table 30 presents the distribution of tabulations, all in the area of "Zionism is impractical."

**Table 30
Distribution for
Zionism Tabulations**

Zionism Tabulations	Israeli	Arab	Total
Number	0	4	4
Percentage	0.0	100.0	100.0
Tabulations per article	0.0	.21	.21
Most in any one day	0	2	

The *News* considered international Zionism impractical since it was thought to be one of the forces behind Israeli aggression.

> The Israeli aggressors, supported by the imperialist forces and international Zionism, seek to overthrow the progressive regimes in the Arab countries and to keep the Middle East in an explosive state which they need to effect their far reaching expansionist designs ("Firm Support," Oct. 20, 1973).

> The government of Israel, supported by external imperialist forces and International Zionist circles, heeded not the voice of the broad international public and aspired once again by military might to impose upon this region of the world the kind of order it desires ("Resolute Protest," Oct. 20, 1973).

> Israeli Zionists, who get broad military support from outside, [desire] to seize more Arab territory ("For Lasting Peace," Nov. 10, 1973).

The fourth tabulation corresponded to a statement that criticized Zionist propaganda. Three of the nineteen articles (15.8 percent) contained at least one tabulation for the category.

Action Justification

There were eighteen tabulations in the area of Arab Action Justification, representing 5.4 percent of the total. Only Peace Seeking, Culpability, and Zionism had as few or fewer tabulations. Table 31 presents the distribution of data, with all eighteen of the tabulations in the area of Arab Action Justification.

Table 31
Distribution for
Action Justification Tabulations

Action Justif. Tabulations	Israeli	Arab	Total
Number	0	18	18
Percentage	0.0	100.0	100.0
Tabulations per article	0.0	.95	.95
Most in any one day	0	3	

It was apparent not only to themselves but to "all sober minded people" (a phrase often employed by the *Moscow News*) that the actions of the Arab peoples were justified:

> The justness of the Arab States' demands for the withdrawal of the aggressor's troops from all Arab territories occupied in 1967 is recognized by all ("Statement by the Soviet Government," Oct. 20, 1973).

> The Arab states, victims of the aggression, are exercising their right to self-defense and [are] waging a legitimate battle ("Tel Aviv's Recklessness," Oct. 27, 1973).

Phrases such as "just struggle" or "just cause" are typical of those tabulated as Arab Action Justification. Eleven of the nineteen articles (57.9 percent) had at least one tabulation in the area of Arab Action Justification.

Culpability

There were eighteen tabulations in this category, representing 5.4 percent of the total. This represents the same frequency as the Action Justification category, and, as might be expected, Table 32 shows that all eighteen were in the area of Israeli Culpability.

Table 32
Distribution for
Culpability Tabulations

Culpability Tabulations	Israeli	Arab	Total
Number	18	0	18
Percentage	100.0	0.0	100.0
Tabulations per article	.95	0.0	.95
Most in any one day	3	0	

The remarks in the *News* were unequivocal and often very similar. The *Moscow News* plainly considered Israel the guilty party:

> The responsibility for the present development of events in the Middle East and their consequences falls wholly on Israel and those external reactionary circles which constantly encourage Israel in its aggressive ambitions ("Statement by the Soviet Government," Oct. 20, 1973).

> The responsibility for the present development rests wholly and completely on Israel and those foreign reactionary circles which regularly encourage Israel's aggressive aspirations ("Tel Aviv's Recklessness," Oct. 27, 1973).

> They [Israelis] bear full responsibility for the blood again being spilt [sic] in the Middle East ... ("Firm Support," Oct. 20, 1973).

Eleven of the nineteen articles (57.8 percent) had at least one tabulation in the area of Culpability.

Superpower/International Culpability

Nineteen of the 333 tabulations (5.7 percent) were in this area, ranking it seventh among the categories. Table 33 presents the Superpower/International Culpability distributions.

Table 33
Distribution for Superpower/
International Culpability Tabulations

Superpower Culpability Tabulations	Total
Number	19
Percentage	5.7
Tabulations per article	1.0
Most in any one day	7

While it is apparent from Table 34 on the following page that the *News* perceived the United States as the primary guilty party, there were six groupings to which guilt was attributed. These were the United States, the oil monopolies, "imperialist forces," "reactionary circles," "reactionary and imperialist forces," and "outside forces." Guilt was specifically attributed to the United States 42.1 percent of the time, and it is highly probable that the nebulous phrases quoted above are all intended to suggest the United States as well. If this is so, then 94.8 percent of the Culpability tabulations are attributable to the United States. The following quotation is indicative of a statement admonishing reactionary and imperialist forces which suggests the identity of the force. "[Israel is] enjoying the support of the same reactionary and imperialist forces which in Chile, as in Indochina, brutally oppose the forces of peace and progress" ("Denouncement and Support," Oct. 27, 1973).

Table 34
Distribution of Superpower/
International Culpability Tabulations

Culpability	Number	Percentage	Tabulations per article
United States	8	42.1	.42
Imperialists	4	21.0	.21
Reactionaries	2	11.5	.10
Reactionary and imperialist forces	1	5.2	.52
Outside forces	3	15.8	.16
Oil monopolies	1	5.2	.52

There are many statements which explicitly depict the US as a culpable party:

> The United States should immediately cease its supplies to the government of Israel and also end all support enabling Israel to pursue its aggressive, expansionist policies ("Denouncement and Support," Oct. 27, 1973).

In contrast to the role played by the United States, the *Moscow News* perceives the Soviet Union as endeavoring to seek peace.

> The Soviet Union, which maintained close contact with the friendly Arab countries, took every political measure within its power to facilitate an early end to the war and the creation of conditions under which a new outbreak would be excluded so that peace in the Middle East might become permanent and durable ("A Period of Hope and Concern," Nov. 17, 1973).

> The Soviet Union is prepared to and will make its constructive contribution to this cause, peace ("The Road to Peace in the Middle East," Nov. 10, 1973).

It is important to note that the *News* threatened Israel, implying possible Soviet military participation:

> If Israel's ruling circles presume that their actions against peaceful cities and civilian targets in Syria and Egypt will remain unpunished, they are profoundly deluded. Aggression cannot remain unpunished and the aggressor must bear harsh responsibility for his actions ("Tass Statement," Oct. 27, 1973).
>
> The continuation of criminal acts by Israel will lead to grave consequences for Israel itself ("Tass Statement," Oct. 27, 1973).
>
> . . . we have been also considering other possible measures whose adoption the situation may require ("The War in the Middle East Must End," Nov. 3, 1973).

Additionally, the *News* perceives world opinion as supporting the Arab cause. It would seem that with the exception of the United States, the *Moscow News* applauds the attitudes and efforts of others in the world arena:

> . . . Thanks to the collective effort of several countries additional opportunities have opened up for a political settlement in the Middle East ("Undelayed Task," Nov. 24, 1973).
>
> World public opinion resolutely condemns the new aggressive act by Israel ("Tel Aviv's Recklessness," Oct. 20, 1973).
>
> Israel is now seen by the international public as an imprudent aggressor ("For Lasting Peace," Nov. 10, 1973).
>
> The numerous comments in the press abroad describe the Statement ["Statement by the Soviet Government"] as fresh evidence of the support by the USSR of the just cause of the Arab nations. This is particularly true of the press of the Arab countries ("Tel Aviv's Recklessness," Oct. 20, 1973).

Ten of the nineteen articles (52.6 percent) had at least one tabulation in this category.

Part III. The Impact of Oil

There were fifteen tabulations in the Oil category, representing only 4.3 percent of the total. This does not suggest a significant concern for oil matters. It is apparent from Table 35 that oil was not a pervasive issue.

Table 35
Distribution of Total Tabulations
Including the Oil Category*

	Number of Tabulations	Percentage of Total
Oil	15	4.3
Aggression	97	27.9
Imperialism	28	8.1
Land legitimacy	27	7.8
Terrorism	46	13.2
Peace seeking	11	3.1
Illegitimacy	21	6.0
Intransigence	44	12.6
Zionism	4	1.2
Action Justification	18	5.2
Culpability	18	5.2
Superpower Culpability	19	5.5

*Total tabulations = 348.

Only four of the nineteen articles (21.1 percent) had at least one Oil tabulation. This is very low when compared to the average category percentage of 57.4 percent for the *Moscow News*. There was an average of .78 tabulations per article, again very low, particularly in light of the fact that one of the four articles contained twelve Oil tabulations.

The *News* considered the oil action as positive, suggesting that the Arab energy measure compelled objectivity and was a function of Israeli intransigence:

> This measure [the embargo] taken by the Arab States has compelled politicians to take a more solid and objective stand regarding the

Middle East conflict ("Oil Hunger," Dec. 8, 1973).

> ... other states are not at all eager to suffer privations for the reason that Tel Aviv is foully violating the rights of the Arab nations ("Undelayed Task," Nov. 24, 1973).

> It is perfectly clear that the Western fuel crisis is nothing but a product of Israel's unwillingness to abandon its aggression against Arab countries. According to reports, the crisis is nothing to be sneezed at ("Undelayed Task," Nov. 24, 1973).

Oil Over Time

Table 36 presents the data for the Oil category divided into two periods: before and after the Arab oil embargo of November 6. Tables 36 through 57 examine the data in relation to these two time periods, defined as October 6 to November 5, 1973, and November 6 to December 8. All fifteen of the tabulations appear after the fifth of November. This, of course, is to be expected. Table 37 shows the distribution of the nineteen articles in the two periods. The oil factor, as indicated by Tables 38 through 57, had no impact on the perspective of the *News*. Its posture remained fixed and unequivocally pro-Arab throughout.

Table 36
Oil Tabulations Distributed
Over Two Time Periods

Oil Tabulations	Oct. 6 - Nov. 5	Nov. 6 - Dec. 8
Number	0	15
Percentage	0.0	100.0

Table 37
Editorial Frequency Distributed
Over Two Time Periods

Editorials	Oct. 6 - Nov. 5	Nov. 6 - Dec. 8
Number	12	7
Percentage	63.2	36.8

Aggression Over Time

Although there are more tabulations for Aggression in the first than the second time period, this is to be expected given the nature of the category. As Table 39 indicates, both before and after the economic action, every article had at least one Aggression tabulation.

Table 38
Aggression Tabulations
Distributed over Two Time Periods

Category	Oct. 6 - Nov. 5 No.[a]	Pct.[b]	Nov. 6 - Dec. 8 No	Pct.
Israeli	68	.70	29	.30
Arab	0	0.0	0	0.0
Total	68	.70	29	.30

[a]Number of tabulations.
[b]Percentage of tabulations in respective category.

Table 39
Articles in Which at Least One Aggression Tabulation Occurs Over Two Time Periods

Category	Oct. 6 - Nov. 5 No.[a]	Pct.[b]	Nov. 6 - Dec. 8 No	Pct.
Israeli	10	100.0	9	100.0
Arab	0	0.0	0	0.0
Total	10	100.0	9	100.0

[a]Number of articles with at least one Aggression tabulation.
[b]Percentage of articles with at least one tabulation.

Imperialism Over Time

As mentioned earlier, it was alleged Israeli imperialism which was labeled causative in the war. It would make sense then that more tabulations would appear in the initial period when more time would be taken discussing the origins of the military outbreak. The data presented in Tables 40 and 41 can be explained through this reasoning.

Table 40
Imperialism Tabulations Distributed over Two Time Periods

Category	Oct. 6 - Nov. 5 No.[a]	Pct.[b]	Nov. 6 - Dec. 8 No	Pct.
Israeli	22	78.6	6	21.4
Arab	0	0.0	0	0.0
Total	22	78.6	6	21.4

[a]Number of tabulations.
[b]Percentage of tabulations in respective category.

Table 41
Articles in Which at Least One
Imperialism Tabulation Occurs
Over Two Time Periods

Category	Oct. 6 - Nov. 5		Nov. 6 - Dec. 8	
	No.[a]	Pct.[b]	No	Pct.
Israeli	8	80.0	4	44.4
Arab	0	0.0	0	0.0
Total	8	80.0	4	44.4

[a]Number of articles with at least one tabulation.
[b]Percentage of articles with at least one tabulation.

Land Legitimacy Over Time

As Table 42 indicates, there is a frequency difference here but no change at all in philosophy. The slight frequency decrease cannot be attributed to a change in policy, particularly when the statements regarding the positive aspects of oil diplomacy are considered. Table 43 indicates an almost exact correspondence of the percentages of articles in which there was at least one tabulation.

Table 42
Land Legitimacy Tabulations
Distributed over Two Time Periods

Category	Oct. 6 - Nov. 5 No.[a]	Pct.[b]	Nov. 6 - Dec. 8 No	Pct.
Israeli	0	0.0	0	0.0
Arab	17	63.0	10	37.0
Total	17	63.0	10	37.0

[a]Number of tabulations.
[b]Percentage of tabulations in respective category.

Table 43
Articles in Which at Least One
Land Legitimacy Tabulation Occurs
Over Two Time Periods

Category	Oct. 6 - Nov. 5 No.[a]	Pct.[b]	Nov. 6 - Dec. 8 No	Pct.
Israeli	0	0.0	0	0.0
Arab	9	90.0	8	88.9
Total	9	90.0	8	88.9

[a]Number of articles with at least one tabulation.
[b]Percentage of articles with at least one tabulation.

Terrorism Over Time

Given the unequivocal nature of the editorial statements in the *News*, the decrease in tabulations for Terrorism from the first to the second period (see Tables 44 and 45) can only be attributed to a decrease in the number of acts the paper perceived as terrorist. It should be noted that 22 of the 45 tabulations in the first period appeared in a single article.

Table 44
Terrorism Tabulations
Distributed over Two Time Periods

Category	Oct. 6 - Nov. 5 No.[a]	Pct.[b]	Nov. 6 - Dec. 8 No	Pct.
Israeli	45	97.8	1	2.2
Arab	0	0.0	0	0.0
Total	45	97.8	1	2.2

[a]Number of tabulations.
[b]Percentage of tabulations in respective category.

Table 45
Articles in Which at Least One
Terrorism Tabulation Occurs
Over Two Time Periods

Category	Oct. 6 - Nov. 5 No.[a]	Pct.[b]	Nov. 6 - Dec. 8 No	Pct.
Israeli	8	80.0	1	11.1
Arab	0	0.0	0	0.0
Total	8	80.0	1	11.1

[a]Number of articles with at least one tabulation.
[b]Percentage of articles with at least one tabulation.

The tabulations in the remainder of the categories, which are given in Tables 46 through 57, require no discussion. Without exception, they reflect the consistently unilateral perspective of the *News* throughout the two periods.

The energy action of the Arab oil states had absolutely no effect on the communications of the *Moscow News*. Indeed, the *News* considered the energy action a solid diplomatic move which promoted objectivity.

Table 46
Peace Seeking Tabulations
Distributed over Two Time Periods

Category	Oct. 6 - Nov. 5 No.[a]	Pct.[b]	Nov. 6 - Dec. 8 No	Pct.
Israeli	0	0.0	2	100.0
Arab	6	66.6	3	33.3
Total	6	54.5	5	45.5

[a]Number of tabulations.
[b]Percentage of tabulations in respective category.

Table 47
Articles in Which at Least One
Peace Seeking Tabulation Occurs
Over Two Time Periods

Category	Oct. 6 - Nov. 5 No.[a]	Pct.[b]	Nov. 6 - Dec. 8 No	Pct.
Israeli	0	0.0	2	22.2
Arab	3	30.0	2	22.2
Total	3	30.0	2	22.2

[a]Number of articles with at least one tabulation.
[b]Percentage of articles with at least one tabulation.

Table 48
Illegitimacy Tabulations
Distributed over Two Time Periods

Category	Oct. 6 - Nov. 5 No.[a]	Pct.[b]	Nov. 6 - Dec. 8 No	Pct.
Israeli	11	52.4	10	47.6
Arab	0	0.0	0	0.0
Total	11	52.4	10	47.6

[a]Number of tabulations.
[b]Percentage of tabulations in respective category.

Table 49
Articles in Which at Least One
Illegitimacy Tabulation Occurs
Over Two Time Periods

Category	Oct. 6 - Nov. 5 No.[a]	Pct.[b]	Nov. 6 - Dec. 8 No	Pct.
Israeli	6	60.0	7	77.8
Arab	0	0.0	0	0.0
Total	6	60.0	7	77.8

[a]Number of articles with at least one tabulation.
[b]Percentage of articles with at least one tabulation.

Table 50
Intransigence Tabulations
Distributed over Two Time Periods

Category	Oct. 6 - Nov. 5 No.[a]	Pct.[b]	Nov. 6 - Dec. 8 No	Pct.
Israeli	25	56.8	19	43.2
Arab	0	0.0	0	0.0
Total	25	56.8	19	43.2

[a]Number of tabulations.
[b]Percentage of tabulations in respective category.

Table 51
Articles in Which at Least One
Intransigence Tabulation Occurs
Over Two Time Periods

Category	Oct. 6 - Nov. 5 No.[a]	Pct.[b]	Nov. 6 - Dec. 8 No	Pct.
Israeli	8	80.0	9	100.0
Arab	0	0.0	0	0.0
Total	8	80.0	9	100.0

[a]Number of articles with at least one tabulation.
[b]Percentage of articles with at least one tabulation.

Table 52
Zionism Tabulations
Distributed over Two Time Periods

Category	Oct. 6 - Nov. 5 No.[a]	Pct.[b]	Nov. 6 - Dec. 8 No	Pct.
Israeli	2	50.0	2	50.0
Arab	0	0.0	0	0.0
Total	2	50.0	2	50.0

[a]Number of tabulations.
[b]Percentage of tabulations in respective category.

Table 53
Articles in Which at Least One
Zionism Tabulation Occurs
Over Two Time Periods

Category	Oct. 6 - Nov. 5 No.[a]	Pct.[b]	Nov. 6 - Dec. 8 No	Pct.
Israeli	0	0.0	0	0.0
Arab	2	20.0	1	11.1
Total	2	20.0	1	11.1

[a]Number of articles with at least one tabulation.
[b]Percentage of articles with at least one tabulation.

Table 54
Action Justification Tabulations
Distributed over Two Time Periods

Category	Oct. 6 - Nov. 5 No.[a]	Pct.[b]	Nov. 6 - Dec. 8 No	Pct.
Israeli	0	0.0	0	0.0
Arab	12	66.6	6	33.3
Total	12	66.6	6	33.3

[a]Number of tabulations.
[b]Percentage of tabulations in respective category.

Table 55
Articles in Which at Least One
Action Justification Tabulation Occurs
Over Two Time Periods

Category	Oct. 6 - Nov. 5 No.[a]	Pct.[b]	Nov. 6 - Dec. 8 No	Pct.
Israeli	0	0.0	0	0.0
Arab	6	60.0	5	55.6
Total	6	60.0	5	55.6

[a]Number of articles with at least one tabulation.
[b]Percentage of articles with at least one tabulation.

Table 56
Culpability Tabulations
Distributed over Two Time Periods

Category	Oct. 6 - Nov. 5 No.a	Oct. 6 - Nov. 5 Pct.b	Nov. 6 - Dec. 8 No	Nov. 6 - Dec. 8 Pct.
Israeli	15	83.3	3	16.7
Arab	0	0.0	0	0.0
Total	15	83.3	3	16.7

aNumber of tabulations.
bPercentage of tabulations in respective category.

Table 57
Articles in Which at Least One
Culpability Tabulation Occurs
Over Two Time Periods

Category	Oct. 6 - Nov. 5 No.a	Oct. 6 - Nov. 5 Pct.b	Nov. 6 - Dec. 8 No	Nov. 6 - Dec. 8 Pct.
Israeli	8	80.0	3	33.3
Arab	0	0.0	0	0.0
Total	8	80.0	3	33.3

aNumber of articles with at least one tabulation.
bPercentage of articles with at least one tabulation.

Part IV. Summary: *The Moscow News*

The *Moscow News* was pro-Arab in philosophy. This is clearly illustrated in Table 58. Of the 312 total tabulations in the bipolar categories, 310 (99.4 percent) were pro-Arab and only two (0.6 percent) were pro-Israeli.

Table 58
Overall Tabulations

	Pro-Israeli	Pro-Arab
Aggression	0	97
Imperialism	0	28
Land legitimacy	0	27
Terrorism	0	46
Peace seeking	2	9
Illegitimacy	0	21
Intransigence	0	44
Zionism	0	4
Action justif.	0	18
Culpability	0	18
Total	2	312
Percentage of total	.6	99.4

The analysis of the *Moscow News* reveals the following perceptions:

1. The Israelis were the aggressors.
2. The Palestinians have the right to the occupied territories.
3. The Arabs made significant initiatives to secure peace.
    a. The only peace initiatives taken by the Israelis were those that were made concurrently with the Arab countries.
    b. The Soviet Union sought peace.
    c. World opinion supports the Arab nations.
4. The Israelis frustrated and sabotaged peace efforts.
5. a. The United States exacerbated the conflict by urging Israel to pursue its aggressive ambitions.
   b. The United States supplied military weapons which escalated the war.

6. The oil policy compelled objectivism.
7. The cause of the war was Israel's expansionist political philosophy.
8. Israel used terrorist tactics.
9. International Zionism served as a catalyst for Israeli aggression.
10. The *Moscow News* did not alter its editorial stance as a result of the oil embargo.

Chapter 5

THE STRAITS TIMES

Part I. Nature of Editorials

Editorials in Singapore's *Straits Times* are defined as those articles appearing on the editorial page under the *Straits Times* bannerhead. These pieces are usually found on page ten of the newspaper. In addition, articles by Ernest Corea have been considered. Corea is a member of the editorial board, and frequently authors "The World," an editorial column.

There were twenty-nine articles in the period covered which dealt either directly or peripherally with the Middle East conflict, and these are the ones referred to henceforth as editorials. Editorials appeared on 48.3 percent of the days from October 6 to December 8, 1973. This averages out to .48 editorials per day, each editorial averaging 487 words. There were approximately 14,100 words written relating either directly or peripherally to the Middle East situation. There was a grand total of 169 tabulations made, ninety-eight of which were in categories other than Oil. These ninety-eight will be considered the total in the next section of this chapter as the Oil category will be discussed separately.

The articles in the *Straits Times* averaged 3.31 tabulations each, and there was an average of .007 tabulations per word.

Part II. Perspectives on Key Issues

Aggression

The Aggression tabulations represented the second greatest frequency among the bipolar categories, with 15.3 percent of the total. Table 59 presents the frequency and percentage of total tabulations for each of the categories.

Table 59
Frequency and Percentage of
Total Tabulations for Each Category*

Category	Israeli No.	Pct.	Arab No.	Pct.	Total No	Pct.
Aggression	3	3.1	12	12.2	15	15.3
Imperialism	0	0.0	0	0.0	0	0.0
Land legitimacy	7	7.1	7	7.1	14	14.2
Terrorism	1	1.0	0	0.0	1	1.0
Peace seeking	8	8.2	14	14.3	22	22.5
Illegitimacy	0	0.0	0	0.0	0	0.0
Intransigence	3	3.1	5	5.1	8	8.2
Zionism	0	0.0	0	0.0	0	0.0
Action justification	0	0.0	1	1.0	1	1.0
Culpability	0	0.0	0	0.0	0	0.0
Superpower culpability					37	37.8

*N = 98.

Table 60 presents the distribution of Aggression tabulations, showing three (20 percent) in the area of Israeli Aggression and twelve (80 percent) in the area of Arab Aggression.

**Table 60
Distribution for
Aggression Tabulations**

Aggression Tabulations	Israeli	Arab	Total
Number	3	12	15
Percentage	20.0	80.0	100.0
Tabulations per article	.10	.41	.51
Most in any one day	1	6	

The *Straits Times* perceived the Arabs to be the aggressors, describing the outbreak as "an assault on two fronts by the Egyptians and Syrians" ("Another War," Oct. 8, 1973). The *Straits Times* writes further:

> Egyptian forces crossed the Suez Canal at five points and established bridgeheads in the Israeli occupied Sinai Peninsula. Similarly, 400 miles to the Northeast, Syrian troops and tanks supported by heavy artillery penetrated at two points into the Israeli occupied Golan Heights ("Another War," Oct. 8, 1973).

It is apparent that the *Times* perceived the Arab nations as initiating the 1973 war. They write straightforwardly: "Egypt and Syria waged war against Israel" ("Getting to the Core of the Arab-Israeli Conflict," Oct. 14, 1973). The only tabulations for Israeli Aggression occurred when both parties were labeled belligerents. Three of the 29 articles (10.3 percent) had at least one tabulation for Israeli Aggression. Six articles (20.7 percent) had at least one tabulation for Arab Aggression. (See Table 61.) As indicated by its relatively high frequency of occurrence, Aggression was considered an important focus of contention in the conflict.

Table 61
Frequency and Percentage of Editorials Containing at Least One Tabulation for Each Category

Category	Israeli No.[a]	Israeli Pct.[b]	Arab No.	Arab Pct.	Total No	Total Pct.
Aggression	3	10.3	6	20.7	6	20.7
Imperialism	0	0.0	0	0.0	0	0.0
Land legitimacy	7	24.1	7	24.1	7	24.1
Terrorism	1	3.5	0	0.0	1	3.5
Peace seeking	6	20.7	13	44.8	13	44.8
Illegitimacy	0	0.0	0	0.0	0	0.0
Intransigence	3	10.3	4	13.8	6	20.7
Zionism	0	0.0	0	0.0	0	0.0
Action justif.	0	0.0	1	3.5	1	3.5
Culpability	0	0.0	0	0.0	0	0.0
Superpowers					13	44.8

[a]Number of editorials with at least one tabulation. There were 29 total editorials.
[b]Percentage of total editorials with at least one tabulation.

Land Legitimacy

Of the total tabulations, 14.2 percent were in the category of Land Legitimacy, ranking it third among the bipolar categories. Table 62 presents the distributions, showing that half the statements were for Arab Land Legitimacy and half for Israeli Land Legitimacy.

Table 62
Distribution for
Land Legitimacy Tabulations

Land Legitimacy Tabulations	Israeli	Arab	Total
Number	7	7	14
Percentage	50.0	50.0	100.0
Tabulations per article	.24	.24	.48
Most in any one day	1	1	

The *Straits Times* supported Israel's right to exist as well as the need to recognize Palestinian rights. Its attitude toward the occupied territory seemed to indicate Arab Legitimacy for these territories. However, they were often vague in speaking of their philosophy on this issue. For example, on October 19, the *Times* writes:

> There is no reason why the United States cannot be committed to Israel's right to exist and simultaneously to redressing Arab grievances. Both are just causes ("The Oil Gambit," Oct. 19, 1973).

What is meant by Arab grievances is difficult to ascertain. Some form of restoration of Palestinian rights must be intended, because the *Times* repeatedly mentions the need for Israel to accept Palestinian rights. On October 20, for example, the *Times* advocates "Arab recognition of Israel's right to existence and Israel's acceptance of Palestinian rights" ("Trying Again?" Oct. 20, 1973). It is not clear whether Palestinian rights mean legitimacy regarding the occupied territory. The *Times* does advocate the implementation of UN Resolution 242, which would indicate such legitimacy, but admits that there are various possible interpretations of the resolution and does not clarify its own interpretation.

In brief, although indefinite regarding particulars, the *Straits Times* supports some form of Palestinian Land Legitimacy in the occupied territories in addition to

Israel's right to exist. Seven of the twenty-nine articles (24.1 percent) contained at least one tabulation for each subcategory.

Terrorism

There was only one tabulation in this area, corresponding to a statement regarding Israeli guerrilla fighters in the 1948 war.

Peace Seeking

The Peace Seeking category had the highest frequency of tabulation of the bipolar categories (22.5 percent). Table 63 presents the distribution.

**Table 63
Distribution for
Peace Seeking Tabulations**

Peace Seeking Tabulations	Israeli	Arab	Total
Number	8	14	22
Percentage	36.4	63.6	100.0
Tabulations per article	.28	.48	.76
Most in any one day	2	2	

Almost two-thirds (63.6 percent) of the tabulations were in the area of Arab Peace Seeking. Many of the tabulations concerned mutual efforts made toward securing peace. Additionally, there were statements regarding Arab Peace Seeking efforts which did not include concurrent Israeli gestures. One such statement concerned an Arab emissary who presented United States President Nixon with a peace proposal ("The Oil Gambit," Oct. 19, 1973). Another centered around efforts President Sadat was making "to take the Middle East stalemate off dead center" ("Trying Again?" Oct. 9, 1973). Six of the 29 twenty-nine articles (20.7 percent) had at least one tabulation for Israeli Peace Seeking, and thirteen (44.8 percent) at least one for Arab Peace Seeking. Apparently, Peace Seeking was perceived as a major issue by the *Times*.

Intransigence

Eight (8.2 percent) of the total tabulations were in the area of Intransigence, five under Arab and three under Israeli Intransigence. The distribution can be seen in Table 64.

Table 64
Distribution for
Intransigence Tabulations

Intransigence Tabulations	Israeli	Arab	Total
Number	3	5	8
Percentage	37.5	62.5	100.0
Tabulations per article	.10	.17	.27
Most in any one day	1	2	

The *Times* did not ascribe a greater level of intransigence to either party. Regarding unwillingness to compromise, the *Times* writes:

> Egypt and Israel are so obsessed with the possibility of battlefield gains, so securely held in thrall by their own emotions, that they may not realize how they are damaging their own cause. Syria and Iraq, smarting under the humiliation of Israel's push on the Golan Heights, have been particularly stubborn. Palestinians predictably disdain the ceasefire ("Crucial Test," Oct. 24, 1973).

> Given the post-'67 combination of Arab frustration and Israeli intransigence, another

round of fighting was inevitable" ("Getting to the Core of the Arab-Israeli Conflict," Oct. 14, 1973).

Three of the twenty-nine articles (10.3 percent) had at least one tabulation for Israeli Intransigence, four (13.8 percent) at least one for Arab Intransigence.

Action Justification

There was only one tabulation in this category, a reference to justification for the Arab oil embargo:

> ... a people who have failed with other means have reason to resort to the ultimate leverage available in their search for justice ("Deadly Weapon," Nov. 29, 1973).

Superpower/International Culpability

The greatest percentage of tabulations among the categories discussed in this section appeared in the Superpower/International Culpability category (see Table 65).

Table 65
Distribution for Superpower/
International Culpability Tabulations

Superpower Culpability	Total
Number	37
Percentage of total	37.8
Tabulations per article	1.27
Most in any one day	12

The *Straits Times*, unquestionably, perceived the superpowers as the guilty parties, repeatedly referring to the war as a proxy war. The *Times* felt that the conflict between Israelis and Arabs was being used by the superpowers.

> It has taken a week for a holy war to be shown up as a "proxy war." For despite the

tribal, legal and humanitarian questions involved in the Middle East conflict, the fact is that today, combatants in the fourth Arab-Israeli war are holding on desperately for the "national interests" of the two super powers, the United States and the Soviet Union ("A Proxy War," Oct. 15, 1973).

The immediate resolution of the conflict . . . lies with the super powers. They can douse the blaze or let the flames roar until one super power is satisfied it has destroyed the other's influence. Arab and Israeli lives will be sacrificed, meanwhile ("A Proxy War," Oct. 15, 1973).

Super power missiles, bombs, tanks, and guns have killed Arabs and Israelis--not Russians and Americans, of course, despite the earlier proclamations of peaceful intent in Moscow and Washington ("Trying Again?" Oct. 20, 1973).

Additionally, the United Nations is admonished by the *Straits Times:*

. . . UN delegates discussing the Middle East . . . seemed remarkably willing to get sidetracked into a discussion of the byproducts of war rather than try to stop the war itself. This may not be accidental. Futile hand-wringing and truculence have paralyzed the Security Council and that could be precisely what partisans in the Middle East conflict want--in the hope that what is now an indecisive battle will eventually turn in favor of "their side." That will be the time for stirring resolutions and ceasefire proposals when diplomatic and military dividends have been secured ("Perilous Delay," Oct. 11, 1973).

All of the Superpower Culpability tabulations except the one quoted above attributed guilt specifically to the superpowers, most referring to the war as a proxy or client war. Thirteen of the 29 articles (44.8 percent) contained at least one tabulation for Superpower/International Culpability.

Culpability, Zionism, and Illegitimacy

There were no tabulations in any of the 29 articles for Arab or Israeli Culpability or Illegitimacy of land holdings. Additionally, there were no tabulations in the category concerned with the practicality or impracticality of Zionism.

Part III. The Impact of Oil

There were seventy-one tabulations in the Oil category, representing 42 percent of the total and almost twice as many as any other category in the study. This frequency would indicate a concern for the oil issue. Table 66 presents the frequency and percentage of the total tabulations for each category in the study.

Table 66
Distribution of Tabulations
Including the Oil Category

Category	Number	Percent
Oil	71	42.0
Aggression	15	8.9
Imperialism	0	0.0
Land legitimacy	14	8.3
Terrorism	1	0.6
Peace seeking	22	13.0
Illegitimacy	0	0.0
Intransigence	8	4.7
Zionism	0	0.0
Action justif.	1	0.6
Culpability	0	0.0
Superpower/International Culpability	37	21.9

It is apparent that oil was an important issue. Four times in the period under examination, there were more than ten tabulations in the category, and twelve of the twenty-nine articles (41.3 percent) had at least one tabulation in the Oil category.

The attitude toward the oil embargo was neutral. Although it is referred to in editorial titles as "The Oil Gambit" and "Deadly Weapon," there is nothing in the editorials to suggest that the *Times* considered the act blackmail. For example, the statement cited in the previous Action Justification section condoning the oil action appears in "Deadly Weapon." The *Times*, however, does caution in that article, "It should be remembered . . . that the overuse of a powerful weapon can be disastrous"

("Deadly Weapon," Nov. 29, 1973), but this is the extent to which the policy is disparaged.

The Oil Factor

As Tables 67 and 68 indicate, there was no unusual effect on either the frequency of tabulations in the Oil category or the number of articles in either period. There were more tabulations in the Oil category after November 6, as would be expected, and there were more articles written regarding the conflict prior to November 6 than after November 6. This makes sense since the war was one month old as of that date. A review of the tabulation data in Tables 69 through 76 will reveal that the oil action made little or no impact on the positions taken by the newspaper vis a vis the bipolar categories. Most of the tabulations appeared in the first month as would be expected, and the frequency of appearance was also greatest in the first month, as would be expected.

Table 67
Oil Tabulations Distributed
Over Two Time Periods

Oil Tabulations	Oct. 6 - Nov. 5	Nov. 6 - Dec. 8
Number	19	52
Percentage	26.8	73.2

Table 68
Editorial Frequency Distributed
Over Two Time Periods

Editorials	Oct. 6 - Nov. 5	Nov. 6 - Dec. 8
Number	17	12
Percentage	58.6	41.4

Table 69
Aggression Tabulations
Distributed over Two Time Periods

Category	Oct. 6 - Nov. 5 No.[a]	Oct. 6 - Nov. 5 Pct.[b]	Nov. 6 - Dec. 8 No	Nov. 6 - Dec. 8 Pct.
Israeli	3	100.0	0	0.0
Arab	12	100.0	0	0.0
Total	15	100.0	0	0.0

[a]Number of tabulations.
[b]Percentage of tabulations in respective category.

Table 70
Articles in Which at Least One
Aggression Tabulation Occurs
Over Two Time Periods

Category	Oct. 6 - Nov. 5 No.[a]	Oct. 6 - Nov. 5 Pct.[b]	Nov. 6 - Dec. 8 No	Nov. 6 - Dec. 8 Pct.
Israeli	3	17.6	0	0.0
Arab	6	35.3	0	0.0
Total	6	35.3	0	0.0

[a]Number of articles with at least one tabulation.
[b]Percentage of articles with at least one tabulation.

Table 71
Land Legitimacy Tabulations
Distributed over Two Time Periods

Category	Oct. 6 - Nov. 5 No.[a]	Pct.[b]	Nov. 6 - Dec. 8 No	Pct.
Israeli	6	85.7	1	14.3
Arab	6	85.7	1	14.3
Total	12	85.7	2	14.3

[a]Number of tabulations.
[b]Percentage of tabulations in respective category.

Table 72
Articles in Which at Least One
Land Legitimacy Tabulation Occurs
Over Two Time Periods

Category	Oct. 6 - Nov. 5 No.[a]	Pct.[b]	Nov. 6 - Dec. 8 No	Pct.
Israeli	6	35.3	1	8.3
Arab	6	35.3	1	8.3
Total	6	35.3	1	8.3

[a]Number of articles with at least one tabulation.
[b]Percentage of articles with at least one tabulation.

Table 73
**Peace Seeking Tabulations
Distributed over Two Time Periods**

Category	Oct. 6 - Nov. 5 No.[a]	Pct.[b]	Nov. 6 - Dec. 8 No	Pct.
Israeli	2	25.0	6	75.0
Arab	9	64.3	5	35.7
Total	11	50.0	11	50.0

[a]Number of tabulations.
[b]Percentage of tabulations in respective category.

Table 74
**Articles in Which at Least One
Peace Seeking Tabulation Occurs
Over Two Time Periods**

Category	Oct. 6 - Nov. 5 No.[a]	Pct.[b]	Nov. 6 - Dec. 8 No	Pct.
Israeli	2	11.8	4	33.3
Arab	9	52.9	4	33.3
Total	9	52.9	4	33.3

[a]Number of articles with at least one tabulation.
[b]Percentage of articles with at least one tabulation.

Table 75
Intransigence Tabulations
Distributed over Two Time Periods

Category	Oct. 6 - Nov. 5 No.[a]	Pct.[b]	Nov. 6 - Dec. 8 No	Pct.
Israeli	2	66.7	1	33.3
Arab	5	100.0	0	0.0
Total	7	87.5	1	12.5

[a]Number of tabulations.
[b]Percentage of tabulations in respective category.

Table 76
Articles in Which at Least One
Intransigence Tabulation Occurs
Over Two Time Periods

Category	Oct. 6 - Nov. 5 No.[a]	Pct.[b]	Nov. 6 - Dec. 8 No	Pct.
Israeli	2	11.7	1	8.3
Arab	4	23.5	0	0.0
Total	5	29.4	1	8.3

[a]Number of articles with at least one tabulation.
[b]Percentage of articles with at least one tabulation.

Part IV. Summary: *The Straits Times*

As Table 77 indicates, the *Straits Times* was balanced in its coverage of the Arab-Israeli war. There was a difference in only three tabulations in the overall dichotomy. Of the tabulations, 52.5 percent were pro-Israel and 47.5 percent were pro-Arab.

Table 77
Overall Tabulations

	Pro-Israeli	Pro-Arab
Aggression	12	3
Imperialism	0	0
Land legitimacy	7	7
Terrorism	0	1
Peace seeking	8	14
Illegitimacy	0	0
Intransigence	5	3
Zionism	0	0
Action justif.	0	1
Culpability	0	0
Total	32	29
Percentage of total	52.5	47.5

The analysis of the *Straits Times* reveals that its editorial perceptions were as follows:

1. The Arabs were the aggressors.
2. a. Israel has a right to survive.
   b. Palestinians have land rights that need to be addressed.
3. The Arabs took more initiatives to secure peace than did the Israelis.
4. Both the Arabs and the Israelis were intransigent at times.
5. The Middle East War was a proxy war for the superpowers.
6. Oil diplomacy can be condoned, but should not be overemployed.
7. The *Straits Times* did not alter its communications as a result of the Arab oil action.

Chapter 6

THE DAILY GRAPHIC

Part I. Nature of Editorials

Editorials in Ghana's *Daily Graphic* are defined as those articles appearing under the heading "Graphic Views," usually found on page two of the newspaper. There were seven articles, all on separate days, dealing with the Middle East conflict, and these will be the editorials referred to in this section. Seven days represent 11.7 percent of the period under study, for an average of .12 editorials per day, each editorial averaging 735.6 words. There were approximately 5,150 words written relating directly or peripherally to the Middle East situation. A total of 97 tabulations were made, 80 of which were in categories other than Oil. These 80 tabulations will be considered the total in the section discussing non-oil related editorials. The oil issue will be dealt with separately. There were 11.4 tabulations per article in the *Daily Graphic* and .02 tabulations per word.

Part II. Perspectives on Key Issues

Aggression

Aggression tabulations represented the greatest frequency among the bipolar categories, with 20 percent of the total. Table 78 presents the frequency and percentage of total tabulations for each of the categories.

Table 78
Frequency and Percentage of Total Tabulations for Each Category*

Category	Israeli No.	Pct.	Arab No.	Pct.	Total No	Pct.
Aggression	16	20.0	0	0.0	16	20.0
Imperialism	10	12.5	0	0.0	10	12.5
Land legitimacy	1	1.2	7	8.8	8	10.0
Terrorism	3	3.7	0	0.0	3	3.7
Peace seeking	0	0.0	2	2.5	2	2.5
Illegitimacy	10	12.5	0	0.0	10	12.5
Intransigence	11	13.8	0	0.0	11	13.8
Zionism	0	0.0	4	5.0	4	5.0
Action justif.	0	0.0	5	6.3	5	6.3
Culpability	3	3.8	0	0.0	3	3.8
Superpowers					8	10.0

*N = 80.

As the table shows, the Aggression category had at least five more tabulations than any other category. Table 79 presents the distribution of the Aggression tabulations, all of which are in the area of Israeli Aggression.

Table 79
Distribution for
Aggression Tabulations

Aggression Tabulations	Israeli	Arab	Total
Number	16	0	16
Percentage	100.0	0.0	100.0
Tabulations per article	2.29	0.0	2.29
Most in any one day	11	0	

It is apparent that the *Daily Graphic* considered the Israelis the aggressor in the conflict, as it explicitly characterizes the war as one "started by Israel" ("War in the Middle East," Oct. 8, 1973), and the Egyptians as victims of aggression:

> As reports indicate, on Saturday, several Israeli Air formations attacked Egyptian troops on the Gulf of Suez which [sic] at the same time, a number of Israeli navy boats approached the Western coast of the Gulf of Suez.
>
> Israel has carried on belligerence which is calculated to show off its unmatched military strength in the whole of the Middle East and to humiliate the beleaguered Arabs and taunt them ("War in the Middle East," Oct. 8, 1973).

Three of the seven days (42.9 percent) had at least one tabulation in the area of Israeli Aggression. Table 80 presents the frequency and percentage of articles in each category for which there was at least one tabulation.

Table 80
Frequency and Percentage of Editorials Containing at Least One Tabulation for Each Category

Category	Israeli No.[a]	Israeli Pct.[b]	Arab No.	Arab Pct.	Total No	Total Pct.
Aggression	3	42.9	0	0.0	3	42.9
Imperialism	4	57.1	0	0.0	4	57.1
Land legitimacy	1	14.3	5	71.4	5	71.4
Terrorism	3	42.9	0	0.0	3	42.9
Peace seeking	0	0.0	2	28.6	2	28.6
Illegitimacy	5	71.4	0	0.0	5	71.4
Intransigence	5	71.4	0	0.0	5	71.4
Zionism	0	0.0	3	42.9	3	42.9
Action justif.	0	0.0	3	42.9	3	42.9
Culpability	2	28.6	0	0.0	2	28.6
Superpowers					4	57.1

[a]Number of editorials with at least one tabulation. There were seven total editorials.
[b]Percentage of total editorials with at least one tabulation.

Imperialism

Imperialism ranked in the top five categories, with 12.5 percent of the total tabulations. Table 81 presents the distribution of tabulations, all of which appear in the Israeli column.

Table 81
Distribution for
Imperialism Tabulations

Imperialism Tabulations	Israeli	Arab	Total
Number	10	0	10
Percentage	100.0	0.0	100.0
Tabulations per article	1.43	0.0	1.43
Most in any one day	7	0	

Obviously the *Daily Graphic* considered Israel an expansionist state. Egypt, the *Daily Graphic* claimed, must defend their land "against the expansionist policies of the settler state of Israel" ("War in the Middle East," Oct. 8, 1973). Israel is said to be "engaged in a war of expansion against an African country" ("Lessons from Middle East," Oct. 13, 1973).

Repeatedly, Israel is described as expansionist, having "encouraged mass settlement of immigrant Jews who are allowed to stream into the country in their [sic] numbers on the occupied lands" ("War in the Middle East," Oct. 8, 1973). Four of the seven articles (57.1 percent) contain at least one tabulation for Israeli Imperialism.

Land Legitimacy

There were eight tabulations in the area of Land Legitimacy, representing 10 percent of the total. As shown in Table 82, almost 90 percent of the tabulations were in the area of Arab Land Legitimacy.

Table 82
Distribution for
Land Legitimacy Tabulations

Land Legitimacy Tabulations	Israeli	Arab	Total
Number	1	7	8
Percentage	12.5	87.5	100.0
Tabulations per article	.14	1.0	1.14
Most in any one day	1	2	

It was the *Daily Graphic's* opinion that Palestinian land rights were the key issue in the conflict. On October 20, 1973, the newspaper writes, "Any peace move which excludes the rights of the Palestinians to their land will only be evading the crux of the unrest in the Middle East" ("Peace Moves in the Middle East," Oct. 20, 1973). It was clear that the *Graphic* considered the Arab peoples the rightful owners of occupied territory:

> The Egyptians who have been victims of aggression for the past six years must resist with their lives and defend their God-given land against the expansionist policies of the settler state of Israel. . . . The clear position is that Egypt is fighting alone to recover part of the continent that has been illegally occupied by Israel ("War in the Middle East," Oct. 8, 1973).

The *Daily Graphic's* position regarding Israel's right to exist is not clear. The *Graphic* writes that "It would be in the interest of both the Arabs and Israelis to agree to respect each other's territorial integrity" ("Peace Moves in the Middle East," Oct. 20, 1973). This statement was tabulated as Israeli Land Legitimacy because of the implicit recognition of Israeli territorial integrity. However, in an earlier editorial, the state of Israel had been described as a "settlement in Palestine" made possible by the United States:

Throughout the brief history of Israeli settlement in Palestine, the arrogant behavior of Israel has been possible because of the direct military support it enjoys from the United States ("War in the Middle East," Oct. 8, 1973).

It is difficult to reconcile this statement with the later one regarding mutual respect of territories, so the position of the *Daily Graphic* with regard to Israel's right to exist remains unclear, in spite of the fact that the issue of Land Legitimacy was perceived by them as an important one, mentioned in five of the seven editorial articles (71.4 percent).

Terrorism

There were only three tabulations in this area, or 3.75 percent of the total, making it one of the three lowest categories in frequency. Table 83 shows that all three tabulations were in the Israeli column.

Table 83
Distribution for
Terrorism Tabulations

Terrorism Tabulations	Israeli	Arab	Total
Number	3	0	3
Percentage	100.0	0.0	100.0
Tabulations per article	.43	0.0	.43
Most in any one day	1	0	

The *Daily Graphic* admonishes Israel for purported actions against civilian targets:

> Under the pretext of taking reprisals against Palestinian commando attacks, Israel had conducted air strikes deep into the heart of

Arab countries, even reaching capitals without retaliation from the Arab countries ("War in the Middle East," Oct. 8, 1973).

Israel . . . is now resorting to bombing innocent targets in Syria, causing death to the civilian population ("Lessons from Middle East," Oct. 13, 1973).

The three mentions of terrorism each appeared in separate editorials, so that 42.9 percent of the articles contained a mention of the issue.

Peace Seeking

With only two tabulations (2.5 percent), Peace Seeking was the category least frequently tabulated. Both tabulations were in the area of Arab Peace Seeking. The *Daily Graphic* perceived the Arabs as being peaceful by nature, writing on October 13: "The Arabs . . . have displayed an inherent aversion for war" ("Lessons from Middle East," Oct. 13, 1973). Two of the seven articles (28.6 percent) had a tabulation for Peace Seeking.

Illegitimacy

Land rights were perceived as a crucial issue by the *Daily Graphic*, as was seen in the related area of Land Legitimacy. There were ten tabulations (12.5 percent) in the area of Illegitimacy of Holdings, making it one of the four highest categories in frequency of tabulations. Table 84 shows that all ten were in the area of Israeli Illegitimacy.

Table 84
Distribution for Illegitimacy Tabulations

Illegitimacy Tabulations	Israeli	Arab	Total
Number	10	0.0	10
Percentage	100.0	0.0	100.0
Tabulations per article	1.43	0.0	1.43
Most in any one day	3	0	

It was the *Daily Graphic's* opinion that the Arab countries had the right to the occupied territories, and Israel had no justification for perpetuating the occupation. Five of the seven editorials (71.4 percent) had at least one tabulation for Israeli Illegitimacy of Holdings.

Intransigence

Intransigence had the second highest frequency of tabulation, with eleven, or 13.8 percent of the total 80 tabulations. Again, the distribution is one-sided: Table 85 shows all eleven tabulations in the Israeli column.

Table 85
Distribution for Intransigence Tabulations

Intransigence Tabulations	Israeli	Arab	Total
Number	11	0	11
Percentage	100.0	0.0	100.0
Tabulations per article	1.57	0.0	1.57
Most in any one day	3	0	

The *Daily Graphic* perceived Israel as an arrogant nation which would unconscionably break international pacts.

100 *Mass Communication and International Politics*

> Though the sudden outbreak of the war had taken the world unawares, the war is not unexpected . . . Since the ceasefire was declared after the 1967 war, Israel had . . . blatantly refused to comply with the United Nations Resolutions . . . ("War in the Middle East," Oct. 8, 1973).
>
> Israel has brazenly flouted every United Nations resolution aimed at bringing peace to the Middle East ("War in the Middle East," Oct. 8, 1973).
>
> Israel should note that it is in her own interest to back down from its stubborn arrogance in any future moves to bring peace to the Middle East ("Lessons from Middle East," Oct. 13, 1973).

Five of the seven articles (71.4 percent) had tabulations in this area, reflecting a concern for the area as a key focus of contention.

Zionism

There were four tabulations in the category relating to the practicality or impracticality of Zionism, representing 5.0 percent of the total. Table 86 presents the monodimensional distribution of the tabulations.

Table 86
Distribution for Zionism Tabulations

Zionism Tabulations	Israeli (Zionism is practical)	Arab (Zionism is impractical)	Total
Number	0	4	4
Percentage	0.0	100.0	100.0
Tabulations per article	0	.57	.57
Most in any day	0	2	

It was the *Daily Graphic's* perception that Zionism was essentially a racist philosophy. On October 8, the *Graphic* writes, "Israel thrives on Zionism racism" ("War in the Middle East," Oct. 8, 1973). A few days later they speak of "Zionist support of racism on the African continent" ("Lessons from Middle East," Oct. 13, 1973). Three of the seven articles (42.9 percent) had at least one tabulation regarding the impracticality of Zionism.

Action Justification

Five tabulations representing 6.3 percent of the total were in the category of Action Justification, ranking fifth from the bottom in frequency of tabulations. Table 87 shows that all five were in the area of Arab Action Justification.

Table 87
Distribution for
Action Justification Tabulations

Action Justif. Tabulations	Israeli	Arab	Total
Number	0	5	5
Percentage	0.0	100.0	100.0
Tabulations per article	0	.71	.71
Most in any one day	0	2	

It was the contention of the *Daily Graphic* that the Arabs' actions were necessary: "One does not fight because one will win, but because one must defend one's rights" ("Lessons from Middle East," Oct. 13, 1973). The *Daily Graphic* also justifies Palestinian endeavors to regain their land.

> The world can scarcely be expected to be spared the unpleasant incidents of hijacking of planes--in which the Israelis have joined and excelled themselves ("Peace Moves in the Middle East," Oct. 20, 1973).

Three of the seven articles (42.9 percent) had at least one tabulation for Arab Action Justification.

Culpability

Culpability was another low-frequency category, with three for 3.8 percent of the total. Table 88 shows that all three were in the area of Israeli Culpability.

**Table 88
Distribution for
Culpability Tabulations**

Culpability Tabulations	Israeli	Arab	Total
Number	3	0	3
Percentage	100.0	0.0	100.0
Tabulations per article	.43	0	.43
Most in any one day	2	0	

The *Graphic* position is clear:

> There is now no question that the Arab nations and the Palestinians have suffered too much injustice from Israeli expansionist intentions, and it is the right of Ghana, as it is of anybody else, to condemn the guilty party ("Africa Shuns Israel," Oct. 30, 1973).

Two of the seven articles (28.5 percent) had tabulations in this category.

Superpower/International Culpability

Eight tabulations, or 10 percent of the total, were in the area of Superpower/International Culpability. This category had the fifth highest frequency of tabulation. Table 89 presents the tabulations for this category.

**Table 89
Distribution for Superpower/
International Culpability Tabulations**

Superpower Culpability	Total
Number	8
Percentage	10.0
Tabulations per article	1.14
Most in any one day	3

It was apparent that the *Daily Graphic* perceived the United States as the guilty party in the Middle East conflict, claiming that the US acts only when it is in their own interest:

> If America is eager to "stand for the right of every nation" why is it that America has never intervened militarily for the millions of Africans held in bondage in South Africa, South West Africa and Rhodesia ... It is only where America sees her interests at stake that she intervenes ... America is only seizing on the least pretext to escalate the war in the Middle East in which Israel has appeared badly beaten ("US in Mideast," Oct. 16, 1973).

Seven of the eight tabulations in this category refer to statements attributing guilt to the United States. One statement admonishes both superpowers:

> Both the United States and the Soviet Union seem quite eager to see an end to the war. The change in the attitude of the super powers to bring peace to the Middle East is a more respectable way of intervening in the war than the intransigent manner in which the two have instigated the combatants to fly at one another's throat, with one of them even

threatening to intervene militarily ("Peace Moves in the Middle East," Oct. 20, 1973).

The *Daily Graphic* felt that the government of Ghana acted positively regarding the conflict:

> The Ghana Government broke off diplomatic relations with Israel on Sunday in a manner that is consistent with the thoughtful and dynamic leadership with which the National Redemption Council has been conducting the affairs of the nation ("Africa Shuns Israel," Oct. 30, 1973).

Four of the seven articles (57.1 percent) had at least one tabulation in this area.

Part III. The Impact of Oil

The Oil category accounted for the highest number of tabulations, seventeen of the total ninety-seven tabulations (17.5 percent) Table 90 presents the frequency and percentage of the total tabulations for each category in the study.

Table 90
Distribution of Tabulations
Including the Oil Category

Category	Number	Percent
Oil	17	17.5
Aggression	16	16.5
Imperialism	10	10.3
Land legitimacy	8	8.3
Terrorism	3	3.1
Peace seeking	2	2.1
Illegitimacy	10	10.3
Intransigence	11	11.3
Zionism	4	4.1
Action justif.	5	5.1
Culpability	3	3.1
Superpower/International Culpability	8	8.3

There was only one more tabulation for Oil than for Aggression, the second ranking category, and fifteen of the seventeen tabulations appeared in one editorial. Only three of the seven articles (41.9 percent) had tabulations in this category. This issue, therefore, was not a relatively major area of concern.

The *Daily Graphic's* comments regarding the oil action essentially justified the Arab embargo:

> What reason do we have to oppose brother countries which withdraw their raw materials from those who refuse to see reason? One only wishes there were more "weapons" of this nature if that is the only way to bring sanity to bear on the supporters of racism ("OAU Meeting and Oil Issue," Nov. 15, 1973).

Oil as a Factor

The data presented in Tables 91 and 92 indicate that the oil issue had little effect on the *Daily Graphic* in terms of their interest in the Middle East.

Table 91
Oil Tabulations Distributed
Over Two Time Periods

Oil Tabulations	Oct. 6 - Nov. 5	Nov. 6 - Dec. 8
Number	2	15
Percentage	11.8	88.2

Table 92
Editorial Frequency Distributed
Over Two Time Periods

Editorials	Oct. 6 - Nov. 5	Nov. 6 - Dec. 8
Number	6	1
Percentage	85.7	14.3

A review of the tabulation data as presented in Tables 93 through 112 will reveal that the oil action had little or no impact on the perceptions of the newspaper. As these tables indicate, there was little or no change in philosophy. Most of the tabulations appeared in the first month as would be expected, and the frequency of appearance was greatest in the first month, as would be expected.

Table 93
Aggression Tabulations Distributed over Two Time Periods

Category	Oct. 6 - Nov. 5 No.[a]	Pct.[b]	Nov. 6 - Dec. 8 No	Pct.
Israeli	16	100.0	0	0.0
Arab	0	0.0	0	0.0
Total	16	100.0	0	0.0

[a]Number of tabulations.
[b]Percentage of tabulations in respective category.

Table 94
Articles in Which at Least One Aggression Tabulation Occurs Over Two Time Periods

Category	Oct. 6 - Nov. 5 No.[a]	Pct.[b]	Nov. 6 - Dec. 8 No	Pct.
Israeli	3	50.0	0	0.0
Arab	0	0.0	0	0.0
Total	3	50.0	0	0.0

[a]Number of articles with at least one tabulation.
[b]Percentage of articles with at least one tabulation.

Table 95
Imperialism Tabulations
Distributed over Two Time Periods

Category	Oct. 6 - Nov. 5 No.[a]	Pct.[b]	Nov. 6 - Dec. 8 No	Pct.
Israeli	10	100.0	0	0.0
Arab	0	0.0	0	0.0
Total	10	100.0	0	0.0

[a]Number of tabulations.
[b]Percentage of tabulations in respective category.

Table 96
Articles in Which at Least One
Imperialism Tabulation Occurs
Over Two Time Periods

Category	Oct. 6 - Nov. 5 No.[a]	Pct.[b]	Nov. 6 - Dec. 8 No	Pct.
Israeli	4	66.7	0	0.0
Arab	0	0.0	0	0.0
Total	4	66.7	0	0.0

[a]Number of articles with at least one tabulation.
[b]Percentage of articles with at least one tabulation.

Table 97
Land Legitimacy Tabulations
Distributed over Two Time Periods

Category	Oct. 6 - Nov. 5 No.[a]	Pct.[b]	Nov. 6 - Dec. 8 No	Pct.
Israeli	1	100.0	0	0.0
Arab	7	100.0	0	0.0
Total	8	100.0	0	0.0

[a]Number of tabulations.
[b]Percentage of tabulations in respective category.

Table 98
Articles in Which at Least One
Land Legitimacy Tabulation Occurs
Over Two Time Periods

Category	Oct. 6 - Nov. 5 No.[a]	Pct.[b]	Nov. 6 - Dec. 8 No	Pct.
Israeli	1	16.7	0	0.0
Arab	5	83.3	0	0.0
Total	5	83.3	0	0.0

[a]Number of articles with at least one tabulation.
[b]Percentage of articles with at least one tabulation.

Table 99
Terrorism Tabulations
Distributed over Two Time Periods

Category	Oct. 6 - Nov. 5 No.[a]	Pct.[b]	Nov. 6 - Dec. 8 No	Pct.
Israeli	3	100.0	0	0.0
Arab	0	0.0	0	0.0
Total	3	100.0	0	0.0

[a]Number of tabulations.
[b]Percentage of tabulations in respective category.

Table 100
Articles in Which at Least One
Terrorism Tabulation Occurs
Over Two Time Periods

Category	Oct. 6 - Nov. 5 No.[a]	Pct.[b]	Nov. 6 - Dec. 8 No	Pct.
Israeli	3	50.0	0	0.0
Arab	0	0.0	0	0.0
Total	3	50.0	0	0.0

[a]Number of articles with at least one tabulation.
[b]Percentage of articles with at least one tabulation.

Table 101
Peace Seeking Tabulations
Distributed over Two Time Periods

Category	Oct. 6 - Nov. 5 No.[a]	Pct.[b]	Nov. 6 - Dec. 8 No	Pct.
Israeli	0	0.0	0	0.0
Arab	2	100.0	0	0.0
Total	2	100.0	0	0.0

[a]Number of tabulations.
[b]Percentage of tabulations in respective category.

Table 102
Articles in Which at Least One
Peace Seeking Tabulation Occurs
Over Two Time Periods

Category	Oct. 6 - Nov. 5 No.[a]	Pct.[b]	Nov. 6 - Dec. 8 No	Pct.
Israeli	0	0.0	0	0.0
Arab	2	33.3	0	0.0
Total	2	33.3	0	0.0

[a]Number of articles with at least one tabulation.
[b]Percentage of articles with at least one tabulation.

Table 103
Illegitimacy Tabulations
Distributed over Two Time Periods

Category	Oct. 6 - Nov. 5 No.[a]	Pct.[b]	Nov. 6 - Dec. 8 No	Pct.
Israeli	7	70.0	3	30.0
Arab	0	0.0	0	0.0
Total	7	70.0	3	30.0

[a]Number of tabulations.
[b]Percentage of tabulations in respective category.

Table 104
Articles in Which at Least One
Illegitimacy Tabulation Occurs
Over Two Time Periods

Category	Oct. 6 - Nov. 5 No.[a]	Pct.[b]	Nov. 6 - Dec. 8 No	Pct.
Israeli	4	66.7	1	100.0
Arab	0	0.0	0	0.0
Total	4	66.7	1	100.0

[a]Number of articles with at least one tabulation.
[b]Percentage of articles with at least one tabulation.

Table 105
Intransigence Tabulations
Distributed over Two Time Periods

Category	Oct. 6 - Nov. 5 No.[a]	Pct.[b]	Nov. 6 - Dec. 8 No	Pct.
Israeli	10	90.9	1	9.1
Arab	0	0.0	0	0.0
Total	10	90.0	1	9.1

[a]Number of tabulations.
[b]Percentage of tabulations in respective category.

Table 106
Articles in Which at Least One
Intransigence Tabulation Occurs
Over Two Time Periods

Category	Oct. 6 - Nov. 5 No.[a]	Pct.[b]	Nov. 6 - Dec. 8 No	Pct.
Israeli	4	66.7	1	100.0
Arab	0	0.0	0	0.0
Total	4	66.7	1	100.0

[a]Number of articles with at least one tabulation.
[b]Percentage of articles with at least one tabulation.

114 Mass Communication and International Politics

Table 107
Zionism Tabulations
Distributed over Two Time Periods

Category	Oct. 6 - Nov. 5 No.[a]	Pct.[b]	Nov. 6 - Dec. 8 No	Pct.
Israeli	4	100.0	0	0.0
Arab	0	0.0	0	0.0
Total	4	100.0	0	0.0

[a]Number of tabulations.
[b]Percentage of tabulations in respective category.

Table 108
Articles in Which at Least One
Zionism Tabulation Occurs
Over Two Time Periods

Category	Oct. 6 - Nov. 5 No.[a]	Pct.[b]	Nov. 6 - Dec. 8 No	Pct.
Israeli	0	0.0	0	0.0
Arab	3	50.0	0	0.0
Total	3	50.0	0	0.0

[a]Number of articles with at least one tabulation.
[b]Percentage of articles wit' at least one tabulation.

Table 109
Action Justification Tabulations
Distributed over Two Time Periods

Category	Oct. 6 - Nov. 5 No.[a]	Pct.[b]	Nov. 6 - Dec. 8 No	Pct.
Israeli	0	0.0	0	0.0
Arab	5	100.0	0	0.0
Total	5	100.0	0	0.0

[a]Number of tabulations.
[b]Percentage of tabulations in respective category.

Table 110
Articles in Which at Least One
Action Justification Tabulation Occurs
Over Two Time Periods

Category	Oct. 6 - Nov. 5 No.[a]	Pct.[b]	Nov. 6 - Dec. 8 No	Pct.
Israeli	0	0.0	0	0.0
Arab	3	50.0	0	0.0
Total	3	50.0	0	0.0

[a]Number of articles with at least one tabulation.
[b]Percentage of articles with at least one tabulation.

Table 111
Culpability Tabulations
Distributed over Two Time Periods

Category	Oct. 6 - Nov. 5 No.[a]	Pct.[b]	Nov. 6 - Dec. 8 No	Pct.
Israeli	3	100.0	0	0.0
Arab	0	0.0	0	0.0
Total	3	100.0	0	0.0

[a]Number of tabulations.
[b]Percentage of tabulations in respective category.

Table 112
Articles in Which at Least One
Culpability Tabulation Occurs
Over Two Time Periods

Category	Oct. 6 - Nov. 5 No.[a]	Pct.[b]	Nov. 6 - Dec. 8 No	Pct.
Israeli	2	33.3	0	0.0
Arab	0	0.0	0	0.0
Total	2	33.3	0	0.0

[a]Number of articles with at least one tabulation.
[b]Percentage of articles with at least one tabulation.

Part IV. Summary: *The Daily Graphic*

The *Daily Graphic's* editorials revealed a pro-Arab perspective. Table 113 indicates that seventy-one of the seventy-two tabulations in the bipolar categories (98.6 percent) were pro-Arab.

Table 113
Overall Tabulations

	Pro-Israeli	Pro-Arab
Aggression	0	16
Imperialism	0	10
Land legitimacy	1	7
Terrorism	0	3
Peace seeking	0	2
Illegitimacy	0	10
Intransigence	0	11
Zionism	0	4
Action justif.	0	5
Culpability	0	3
Total	1	71
Percentage of total	1.4	98.6

The analysis of the *Daily Graphic* reveals that its editorial perceptions were as follows:

1. The Israelis were the aggressors.
2. Israel is imperialistic.
3. a. The Arabs have a right to the occupied territories.
   b. Palestinians have land rights and this is the crux of the conflict.
4. The Israelis employed terrorist tactics.
5. The Arab peoples are peace-seeking peoples.
6. Israel has been intransigent regarding efforts to secure peace.
7. Zionism is equivalent to racism.
8. The Arabs are justified in fighting the Israelis.
9. Israel is the guilty party in the conflict.

10. a. America has acted expediently and should be admonished for its role in the dispute.
    b. Both superpowers are culpable because, initially, their policies exacerbated the conflict.
11. Oil, as political diplomacy, is a justifiable weapon.
12. There was no effect at all of the oil weapon on the perceptions of the *Daily Graphic*.

Chapter 7

THE ASAHI EVENING NEWS

Part I. Nature of Editorials

Editorials in Japan's *Asahi Evening News* appear under its bannerhead, usually on page four of the newspaper. In this section, the term editorials will include articles under the bannerhead and the column "Vox Populi, Vox Dei," also appearing on the editorial page. Both of these columns are written by members of the *Asahi Evening News* editorial staff. In the period under study, there were twenty-seven articles dealing either directly or peripherally with the Middle East conflict, appearing on twenty-three separate days (38.3 percent of the period). This represents an average of .45 editorials per day, each editorial averaging 813.9 words, for a total of approximately 21,975 words written relating either directly or peripherally to the Middle East situation. There were 251 tabulations made, sixty-eight in categories other than Oil. Editorials in Oil and non-Oil categories will be discussed separately. The articles in the *Asahi Evening News* averaged 2.51 tabulations each. There were .003 tabulations per word.

Part II. Perspectives on Key Issues

Aggression

There were eleven tabulations, representing 16.2 percent of the total, in the Aggression category. Table 114 provides the totals for each category, showing Aggression ranked third in frequency of occurrence.

Table 114
Frequency and Percentage of Total Tabulations for Each Category*

Category	Israeli No.	Israeli Pct.	Arab No.	Arab Pct.	Total No	Total Pct.
Aggression	6	8.8	5	7.4	11	16.2
Imperialism	7	10.3	0	0.0	7	10.3
Land legitimacy	5	7.4	9	13.2	14	20.6
Terrorism	3	4.4	10	14.7	13	19.1
Peace seeking	1	1.5	5	7.4	6	8.8
Illegitimacy	4	5.8	0	0.0	4	5.8
Intransigence	1	1.5	3	4.4	4	5.8
Zionism	0	0.0	0	0.0	0	0.0
Action justif.	0	0.0	5	7.4	5	7.4
Culpability	0	0.0	0	0.0	0	0.0
Superpowers					4	5.8

*N = 68.

Table 115, below, presents the distribution of the Aggression tabulations, showing that the *Asahi Evening News* perceived both parties to be aggressors.

Table 115
Distribution for Aggression Tabulations

Aggression Tabulations	Israeli	Arab	Total
Number	6	5	11
Percentage	54.6	45.4	100.0
Tabulations per article	.22	.19	.41
Most in any one day	3	3	

Most of the tabulations in this category were recorded when both parties were labeled belligerents, but generally the tone of the statements is mild. There is no condemnation or admonishing of either party. An early sentence in one article states, "It is not clear as to exactly who set the tinder ablaze on Saturday" but goes on to say that ". . . the Arabs become the ones who first pulled the trigger" ("Arab-Israeli Conflict," Oct. 9, 1973). The position seems to be that if the Mideast situation was "tinder" waiting to be lit, it doesn't much matter who did the lighting.

Four of the twenty-seven editorials had at least one tabulation for Israeli Aggression, and three of these also included one for Arab Aggression. Frequency and percentage of tabulations for each category are presented in Table 116. It can be seen in this table that Aggression falls in the mid-range of frequency.

Table 116
Frequency and Percentage of Editorials
Containing at Least One Tabulation
for Each Category

Category	Israeli No.[a]	Pct.[b]	Arab No.	Pct.	Total No	Pct.
Aggression	4	14.8	3	11.1	4	14.8
Imperialism	6	22.2	0	0.0	6	22.2
Land legitimacy	3	11.1	4	14.8	6	22.2
Terrorism	3	11.1	4	14.8	5	18.5
Peace seeking	1	3.7	3	11.1	3	11.1
Illegitimacy	3	11.1	0	0.0	3	11.1
Intransigence	1	3.7	3	11.1	4	14.8
Zionism	0	0.0	0	0.0	0	0.0
Action justif.	0	0.0	4	14.8	4	14.8
Culpability	0	0.0	0	0.0	0	0.0
Superpowers					2	7.4

[a]Number of editorials with at least one tabulation. There were twenty-seven total editorials.
[b]Percentage of total editorial with at least one tabulation.

Imperialism

There were seven tabulations representing 10.3 percent of the total, ranking Imperialism fourth in frequency among the eleven categories. Table 117 presents the distribution for the Imperialism tabulations, all of which are in the area of Israeli Imperialism.

Table 117
Distribution for
Imperialism Tabulations

Imperialism Tabulations	Israeli	Arab	Total
Number	7	0	7
Percentage	100.0	0.0	100.0
Tabulations per article	.26	0.0	.26
Most in any one day	2	0	

The *News* perceived the Israelis to be expanding their boundaries in an imperialistic manner. On October 18, the *News* writes, "Israel should stop giving the Arab side the fear of a military state expanding like cancer cells" ("Middle East War," Oct. 18, 1973). In the same editorial is a reference to the Israeli desire to "perpetuate the occupation." Tabulations in this category refer to the Israeli occupation and settlement of territories occupied since the 1967 war. Six of the twenty-seven articles (22.2 percent) had at least one tabulation in this area.

Land Legitimacy

Land Legitimacy had the greatest percentage of tabulations of all categories, with fourteen tabulations representing 20.6 percent of the total. Table 118 presents the distribution, showing almost two-thirds of the tabulations in the area of Arab rather than Israeli Land Legitimacy.

Table 118
Distribution for
Land Legitimacy Tabulations

Land Legitimacy Tabulations	Israeli	Arab	Total
Number	5	9	14
Percentage	35.7	64.3	100.0
Tabulations per article	.18	.33	.51
Most in any one day	2	4	

The *Asahi Evening News* felt that the occupied territory belonged to the Arab people and that the Israeli argument for the necessity of continued occupation was weak. The *News* writes:

> The Sinai Peninsula and the Golan Heights . . . are Arab territory rather than Israeli territory . . . Can't it [Israel] withdraw its one sided argument that territory taken from other countries is necessary for its own safety ("Middle East Solution," Oct. 25, 1973).

Additionally, the paper commented upon the need for recognition of Palestinian land rights. The entire article of November 5, "For Peace in the Middle East," discussed a possible national home for the Palestinians and, in general, the need to address Palestinian grievances. It is important to note that this addressing of Palestinian grievances according to the *Asahi Evening News* does not include granting land to Palestinians inside the State of Israel. It is not made clear exactly where a Palestinian national state should be, but the position of the *News* is that it should not include the pre-1967 State of Israel.

> Can't the Arabs who have withdrawn their demand for the extermination of Israel go one step further and officially recognize the existence of Israel? ("Middle East Solution," Oct. 25, 1973).

> [T]here is no shadow of an Israel obliterations argument as often advocated by the Arab leaders. If there is even one saving grace in the latest war ... it is the appearance of such new thinking ("Middle East War," Oct. 18, 1973).

In short, the *Asahi Evening News* felt that the occupied territories belonged to the Arab peoples; the Palestinians' rights should be recognized as well as Israel's right to exist. Three of the twenty-seven articles (11.1 percent) contained at least one tabulation for Israeli Land Legitimacy and four (14.8 percent) contained at least one for Arab Land Legitimacy.

Terrorism

Thirteen of the sixty-eight total tabulations were in the area of Terrorism. This represented 19.1 percent of the total and ranked second in frequency among the categories. Table 119 presents the distributions.

Table 119
Distribution for Terrorism Tabulations

Terrorism Tabulations	Israeli	Arab	Total
Number	3	10	13
Percentage	23.1	76.9	100.0
Tabulations per article	.11	.37	.48
Most in any one day	1	4	

Over three-quarters of the tabulations were in the area of Arab Terrorism, but again the editorial tone was mild. The paper mentioned incidents of terrorism such as the KLM hijacking, the Israeli shooting down of a Syrian fighter plane prior to the war, and acts of Arab guerrillas. These incidents were reported rather than held up for condemnation; indeed, at times there was some justification seen for terrorist activities. The paper stated at one point that the absence of a Palestinian settlement forced them to "turn to guerrilla activities" ("For Peace in the Middle East," Nov. 5, 1973). In short there were statements that terrorist acts had taken place, but no statements that these acts were inappropriate. Three of the twenty-seven articles (11.1 percent) mentioned Israeli Terrorism; four (14.8 percent) mentioned Arab Terrorism.

Peace Seeking

There were six tabulations, or 8.8 percent of the total, in the area of Peace Seeking, which ranked fifth in frequency among the categories. Table 120 presents the distribution, which shows almost all tabulations in the Arab Peace Seeking column.

Table 120
Distribution for Peace Seeking Tabulations

Peace Seeking Tabulations	Israeli	Arab	Total
Number	1	5	6
Percentage	16.7	83.3	100.0
Tabulations per article	.03	.19	.22
Most in any one day	1	2	

Clearly, the *Asahi Evening News* felt that the Arabs had made the greater efforts toward attaining peace: "The Arab side continued to make all efforts during these six years to achieve a political solution of the problem" ("The Middle East War," Oct. 18, 1973). The single tabulation for Israeli Peace Seeking corresponds to a statement mentioning mutual acceptance of a ceasefire. Three of the twenty-seven articles (11.1 percent) had tabulations for Arab Peace Seeking; one (3.7 percent) for Israeli Peace Seeking.

Illegitimacy

Illegitimacy, along with the Intransigence and Superpower Culpability categories, had the smallest number of tabulations at four, or 5.8 percent of the total. Table 121 presents the distribution, which was monodimensional.

126 *Mass Communication and International Politics*

Table 121
Distribution for Illegitimacy Tabulations

Illegitimacy Tabulations	Israeli	Arab	Total
Number	4	0	4
Percentage	100.0	0.0	100.0
Tabulations per article	.14	0	.14
Most in any one day	2	0	0

As in the related are of Land Legitimacy, the Illegitimacy tabulations referred to the occupation of territories held by Israel since the 1967 war. Three of the twenty-seven articles (11.1 percent) had at least one tabulation in this area.

Intransigence

Intransigence also had only four tabulations, distributed as shown in Table 122.

Table 122
Distribution for Intransigence Tabulations

Intransigence Tabulations	Israeli	Arab	Total
Number	1	3	4
Percentage	25.0	75.0	100.0
Tabulations per article	.03	.11	.14
Most in any one day	1	1	

The tabulations for Arab Intransigence referred to the adamancy of the oil magnates in dealing with the conflict. An October 20 editorial states:

> When we examine the communique issued by the organization of Arab Petroleum Exporting Countries ... we find no signs that the Arab nations are in too great a hurry to bring about quick settlement to the Arab Israeli conflict ("The Arab Oil War," Oct. 20, 1973).

The sole tabulation for Israeli Intransigence refers to UN Resolution 242, describing the Israelis as having "ignored the resolution" ("The Middle East War," Oct. 18, 1973). This category was not perceived as a major area of contention by the *Asahi Evening News*.

Zionism

There were no tabulations in the category regarding the practicality or impracticality of Zionism in the *Asahi Evening News*.

Action Justification

Action Justification ranked sixth among the categories, with five tabulations or 7.4 percent of the total. Table 123 presents the distribution.

Table 123
Distribution for
Action Justification Tabulations

Action Justif. Tabulations	Israeli	Arab	Total
Number	0	5	5
Percentage	0.0	100.0	100.0
Tabulations per article	0	.18	.18
Most in any one day	0	2	

The tabulations, all in the area of Arab justification, referred to statements that justify the Arab action in light of the Israeli occupation of the territory. The *News* writes on October 9:

> It must have been unbearable for the radical minded Arab military to depend any further on the unreliable method of political settlement as they watched before their very eyes the steady progress being made in Israeli perpetuation of the occupied territory ("Arab Israeli Conflict," Oct. 9, 1973).
>
> The Arab side has continued to make all possible efforts during these six years to achieve a political solution of the problem, but because the attitude of the US which supports Israel did not change, the Arab side has used force to make Israel comply with the UN resolution ("The Middle East War," Oct. 18, 1973).

Four of the twenty-seven articles (14.8 percent) had at least one tabulation in this category.

Culpability

There were no statements in the twenty-seven editorials that were tabulated as Arab or Israeli Culpability. There were some statements intimating culpability, but in these instances the statements were more appropriately tabulated in other categories.

Superpower/International Culpability

This was the third area tied for lowest frequency of tabulations, with only four tabulations (5.9 percent of the total). Table 124 summarizes the tabulations.

Table 124
Distribution for Superpower/
International Culpability Tabulations

Superpower Culpability	Total
Number	4
Percentage	5.9
Tabulations per article	.14
Most in any one day	3

The small number of statements concerning the superpowers might suggest that this was not an area of major concern to the *Asahi Evening News*, but some of the comments made were particularly caustic. The Culpability statements all referred to the US and Soviet Union as the guilty parties. The war was called a proxy war, and the attitude is critical of the superpowers.

> The fourth Middle East War is deepening its aspect as a second Vietnam War in the sense of being a testing ground for new American and Soviet weapons ("The Middle East War," Oct. 18, 1973).

> [T]he measures taken by the United States and the Soviet Union since the war started are none other than deplorable policies which will lead to prolongation of the war ("The Middle East War," Oct. 18, 1973).

> With the use of many new weapons in the fourth Middle East War it gave the appearance of a war by proxy for the East and the West ("For Peace in the Middle East," Nov. 5, 1973).

There were no parties other than the superpowers that were considered culpable in the conflict. Two of the twenty-seven articles (7.4 percent) had tabulations in this category.

Part III. The Impact of Oil

By far the majority of the tabulations, 183 of the total 251, were in the Oil category, as shown in Table 125.

Table 125
Distribution of
Total Tabulations for Each Category
Including the Oil Category*

Category	No.	Pct.
Oil	183	72.9
Aggression	11	4.4
Imperialism	7	2.8
Land legitimacy	14	5.6
Terrorism	13	5.2
Peace seeking	6	2.4
Illegitimacy	4	1.6
Intransigence	4	1.6
Zionism	0	0.0
Action justif.	5	2.0
Culpability	0	0.0
Superpowers	4	1.6

*N = 251.

It is clear that oil was an issue of great concern to the *Asahi Evening News*. Almost all of the twenty-seven articles (92.6 percent) had at least one tabulation in this category, with an average of 6.8 tabulations per editorial. Eight articles had more than ten and two had more than twenty tabulations in this category. Table 126 presents the data for Oil distributed over the two time periods, showing that interest in oil increased after November 6, which is to be expected. However, Table 127 indicates that there were twice as many articles written about the conflict after the embargo than there were before. This is not consistent with what one might expect, for it means that the *Asahi Evening News* evidenced greater interest in the War in the *second* month rather than in the month immediately after the War started. This finding might be explained in part by the fact that ten of the editorials in the second time period, although peripherally related to the Middle East, were primarily concerned with the oil issue.

Table 126
Oil Tabulations Distributed
Over Two Time Periods

Oil Tabulations	Oct. 6 - Nov. 5	Nov. 6 - Dec. 8
Number	59	124
Percentage	32.2	67.8

Table 127
Editorial Frequency Distributed
Over Two Time Periods

Editorials	Oct. 6 - Nov. 5	Nov. 6 - Dec. 8
Number	9	18
Percentage	33.3	66.7

The editorial posture of the *Asahi Evening News* regarding Arab oil policy is somewhat ambivalent. Prior to November 27, 1973, the oil policy is described as a political measure and a potent weapon. The *News* quotes with approval another newspaper's contention that the oil action is:

> a "fourth force" on an equal footing with the three branches of the armed forces--the army, navy and air force.... Saudi Arabia has the mightiest "oil force" on earth ("The Arab Oil War," Oct. 20, 1973).

On November 21, the *News* writes:

> [T]he Arab bloc is out to win the political war by choking the West with oil as its weapon in unfolding an oil-based economic war ("Arab Oil Strategy," Nov. 21, 1973).

On November 24, the *News* wrote sharply after the Japanese government's change in Middle East policy from a neutral to a pro-Arab stand:

> In connection with the Arab-Israel dispute being "neutral" sounds good, but it was in effect a policy of "letting sleeping dogs lie." Everything is all right as long as Japan can buy oil--wasn't this the shabby true nature of Japan's policy towards the Arab countries? ("Japanese Cicada," Nov. 24, 1973).

After November 27, the *News* defends the Japanese government's change in policy and does not characterize the oil measure as a negative force or a choking power. The *News* claims that after November 27, the oil policy enabled the Japanese to view the Middle East crisis more objectively and allowed the government to formulate a policy consistent with independent thinking and international justice. Numerous statements reveal these changed perceptions:

> Today, with conditions for our diplomacy having been made clear due to the oil crisis--a situation in which neither a simple attitude of stand-patism nor diplomatic bargaining based on power politics is permissible--we feel all the more need for an independent diplomacy based on international justice. ("New Mideast Policy," Nov. 27, 1973).

> The Japanese government must grasp the true substance of the Mideast problem by firmly adjusting its sights to the achieving of international justice, and take its own independent course of diplomacy.
> Otherwise, Japan's new Middle East policy will not be spared the criticism that it was formulated out of a mere desire for oil. The Japanese government must not spare any diplomatic efforts in repeatedly explaining Japan's position to the other countries and in securing their understanding ("Japan, US and Oil Pinch," Dec. 5, 1973).

> The announcement of these four principles [mentioned in the Middle East Policy] was

clearly a diplomatic step forward inasmuch as they clarify that the Japanese government has adjusted its diplomatic sights on international justice in line with Japan's Peace Constitution ("Japan, US and Oil Pinch," Dec. 5, 1973).

... by regarding the Middle East problem as Japan's own problem and shedding its erstwhile noncommittal posture, our government has taken diplomatic measures aimed at a settlement of the problem ... Although our country has continued to support Resolution 242 of the UN Security Council for settlement of the Middle East issue, it has failed to make explicit its interpretation of the resolution up till now. Chief Cabinet Secretary Nikaido has raised the point that "seizure and occupation of territory through military force are impermissible" and also, expressed his view that it is only through complete withdrawal by the Israelis that the road to settlement of the dispute will be opened up.

This is a natural course in thinking in the light of our regard for international justice as expressed in Japan's Peace Constitution. That this natural fact could not be made clear until our country was confronted with output restrictions by the Arab oil-producing nations has been the structural weak point of Japanese diplomacy ("New Mideast Policy," Nov. 27, 1973).

... this Middle East policy was decided after taking into consideration, the Japanese national interests as well as the proper diplomatic course, in other words, that even though hesitatingly, this new course was adopted with "our independent thinking" as the core ("New Mideast Policy," Nov. 27, 1973).

Although the attitude toward the oil policy changes, the statements in the *Asahi Evening News* do not reflect a change in any other area regarding the Middle East War.

The Japanese government altered its neutral policy to a pro-Arab stance, but the editorial perceptions of the

News remain the same, with consistent support of the rights of the Palestinians to land, and the assertion that Israeli occupation of the territories was illegal.

In short, the oil embargo did not alter the *News'* perceptions on any issues except the oil issue. It was, however, apparent that there was a greater interest in the Middle East conflict after the embargo than there had been before. This is borne out by the time-period distributions in Tables 128 through 143.

Table 128
Aggression Tabulations
Distributed over Two Time Periods

Category	Oct. 6 - Nov. 5 No.[a]	Pct.[b]	Nov. 6 - Dec. 8 No	Pct.
Israeli	6	100.0	0	0.0
Arab	5	100.0	0	0.0
Total	11	100.0	0	0.0

[a]Number of tabulations.
[b]Percentage of tabulations in respective category.

Table 129
Articles in Which at Least One
Aggression Tabulation Occurs
Over Two Time Periods

Category	Oct. 6 - Nov. 5 No.[a]	Pct.[b]	Nov. 6 - Dec. 8 No	Pct.
Israeli	4	44.0	0	0.0
Arab	3	33.0	0	0.0
Total	4	44.0	0	0.0

[a]Number of articles with at least one tabulation.
[b]Percentage of articles with at least one tabulation.

Table 130
Imperialism Tabulations
Distributed over Two Time Periods

Category	Oct. 6 - Nov. 5 No.[a]	Pct.[b]	Nov. 6 - Dec. 8 No	Pct.
Israeli	3	42.9	4	57.1
Arab	0	0.0	0	0.0
Total	3	42.9	4	57.1

[a]Number of tabulations.
[b]Percentage of tabulations in respective category.

Table 131
Articles in Which at Least One
Imperialism Tabulation Occurs
Over Two Time Periods

Category	Oct. 6 - Nov. 5 No.[a]	Pct.[b]	Nov. 6 - Dec. 8 No	Pct.
Israeli	2	22.2	5	27.8
Arab	0	0.0	0	0.0
Total	2	22.2	5	27.8

[a]Number of articles with at least one tabulation.
[b]Percentage of articles with at least one tabulation.

Table 132
Land Legitimacy Tabulations
Distributed over Two Time Periods

Category	Oct. 6 - Nov. 5 No.[a]	Pct.[b]	Nov. 6 - Dec. 8 No	Pct.
Israeli	4	80.0	1	20.0
Arab	6	66.0	3	33.0
Total	10	71.4	4	28.6

[a]Number of tabulations.
[b]Percentage of tabulations in respective category.

Table 133
Articles in Which at Least One
Land Legitimacy Tabulation Occurs
Over Two Time Periods

Category	Oct. 6 - Nov. 5 No.[a]	Pct.[b]	Nov. 6 - Dec. 8 No	Pct.
Israeli	2	22.2	1	5.6
Arab	2	22.2	2	11.1
Total	3	33.3	3	16.7

[a]Number of articles with at least one tabulation.
[b]Percentage of articles with at least one tabulation.

Table 134
Terrorism Tabulations
Distributed over Two Time Periods

Category	Oct. 6 - Nov. 5 No.[a]	Pct.[b]	Nov. 6 - Dec. 8 No	Pct.
Israeli	1	33.3	2	66.7
Arab	5	50.0	5	50.0
Total	6	41.1	7	53.9

[a]Number of tabulations.
[b]Percentage of tabulations in respective category.

Table 135
Articles in Which at Least One
Terrorism Tabulation Occurs
Over Two Time Periods

Category	Oct. 6 - Nov. 5 No.[a]	Pct.[b]	Nov. 6 - Dec. 8 No	Pct.
Israeli	1	11.1	2	11.1
Arab	2	22.2	2	11.1
Total	2	22.2	3	33.3

[a]Number of articles with at least one tabulation.
[b]Percentage of articles with at least one tabulation.

Table 136
Peace Seeking Tabulations
Distributed over Two Time Periods

Category	Oct. 6 - Nov. 5 No.[a]	Pct.[b]	Nov. 6 - Dec. 8 No	Pct.
Israeli	0	0.0	1	100.0
Arab	1	20.0	4	80.0
Total	1	16.7	5	83.3

[a]Number of tabulations.
[b]Percentage of tabulations in respective category.

Table 137
Articles in Which at Least One
Peace Seeking Tabulation Occurs
Over Two Time Periods

Category	Oct. 6 - Nov. 5 No.[a]	Pct.[b]	Nov. 6 - Dec. 8 No	Pct.
Israeli	0	0.0	1	5.6
Arab	1	11.1	2	11.1
Total	1	11.1	2	11.1

[a]Number of articles with at least one tabulation.
[b]Percentage of articles with at least one tabulation.

Table 138
Illegitimacy Tabulations
Distributed over Two Time Periods

Category	Oct. 6 - Nov. 5 No.[a]	Pct.[b]	Nov. 6 - Dec. 8 No	Pct.
Israeli	1	25.0	3	75.0
Arab	0	0.0	0	0.0
Total	1	25.0	3	75.0

[a]Number of tabulations.
[b]Percentage of tabulations in respective category.

Table 139
Articles in Which at Least One
Illegitimacy Tabulation Occurs
Over Two Time Periods

Category	Oct. 6 - Nov. 5 No.[a]	Pct.[b]	Nov. 6 - Dec. 8 No	Pct.
Israeli	1	11.1	2	11.1
Arab	0	0.0	0	0.0
Total	1	11.1	2	11.1

[a]Number of articles with at least one tabulation.
[b]Percentage of articles with at least one tabulation.

Table 140
Intransigence Tabulations
Distributed over Two Time Periods

Category	Oct. 6 - Nov. 5 No.[a]	Pct.[b]	Nov. 6 - Dec. 8 No	Pct.
Israeli	1	100.0	0	0.0
Arab	2	66.7	1	33.3
Total	3	75.0	1	25.0

[a]Number of tabulations.
[b]Percentage of tabulations in respective category.

Table 141
Articles in Which at Least One
Intransigence Tabulation Occurs
Over Two Time Periods

Category	Oct. 6 - Nov. 5 No.[a]	Pct.[b]	Nov. 6 - Dec. 8 No	Pct.
Israeli	1	11.1	0	0.0
Arab	2	22.2	1	5.6
Total	3	29.4	1	5.6

[a]Number of articles with at least one tabulation.
[b]Percentage of articles with at least one tabulation.

Table 142
Action Justification Tabulations
Distributed over Two Time Periods

Category	Oct. 6 - Nov. 5 No.[a]	Pct.[b]	Nov. 6 - Dec. 8 No	Pct.
Israeli	0	0.0	0	0.0
Arab	4	80.0	1	20.0
Total	4	80.0	1	20.0

[a]Number of tabulations.
[b]Percentage of tabulations in respective category.

Table 143
Articles in Which at Least One
Action Justification Tabulation Occurs
Over Two Time Periods

Category	Oct. 6 - Nov. 5 No.[a]	Pct.[b]	Nov. 6 - Dec. 8 No	Pct.
Israeli	0	0.0	0	0.0
Arab	3	33.3	1	5.6
Total	3	33.3	1	5.6

[a]Number of articles with at least one tabulation.
[b]Percentage of articles with at least one tabulation.

Part IV. Summary: *The Asahi Evening News*

The *Asahi Evening News* was pro-Arab in perspective, as Table 144 reveals. Of the tabulations, 65.6 percent were pro-Arab in philosophy and 34.4 percent were pro-Israeli.

**Table 144
Overall Tabulations**

	Pro-Israeli	Pro-Arab
Aggression	5	6
Imperialism	0	7
Land legitimacy	5	9
Terrorism	10	3
Peace seeking	1	5
Illegitimacy	0	4
Intransigence	1	3
Zionism	0	0
Action justif.	0	5
Culpability	0	0
Total	22	42
Percentage of total	34.4	65.6

The analysis of the *Asahi Evening News* editorials reveals the following perceptions:

1. The Arabs and Israelis were equally aggressive.
2. a. Israel has the right to exist.
   b. The Arabs have a right to the occupied territory.
   c. The Palestinians have legitimate rights that cannot be ignored.
3. The Palestinians and the Israelis employed terrorist tactics.
4. The Arabs took the most initiatives to secure peace.
5. The oil lords were, at times, intransigent.
6. The superpowers were culpable for actions taken in the conflict.

7. a. Oil diplomacy was initially a weapon used to force countries to sympathize with the Arabs.
   b. The oil policy eventually created an atmosphere in which Japan could perceive its international role more objectively.
8. The *Asahi Evening News* did not alter its communications as a result of the oil embargo with the exception of the newspaper's perception of the oil issue itself.

Chapter 8

THE TIMES OF LONDON

Part I. Nature of Editorials

Editorials in the *Times* of London appear under the *Times* bannerhead in the editorial section of the newspaper. Additionally, editorials include articles written in the "Times Diary" section by members of the editorial board. Articles by Victor Zorza, a member of the board, would be included, for example, whereas articles by Louis Heren, a military analyst, were excluded by definition. From this point, the word editorials refers to sixty-three articles which dealt directly or peripherally with the Middle East conflict during the period under study. Of the sixty days in the period, forty-four days (73.3 percent) included such articles, for an average of 1.05 editorials per day. The editorials averaged 887.9 words in length, and there were approximately 55,950 words written either directly or peripherally about the conflict. There were 468 tabulations made in all, 163 of which were in categories other than the Oil category. In the following discussion, these 163 tabulations will be considered the total, and oil will be discussed separately. There was an average of 2.58 tabulations for each article in the *Times* of London and there were .003 tabulations per word.

Part II. Perspectives on Key Issues

Aggression

Aggression had the greatest frequency of tabulations, with forty-one of the 163 total (25.2 percent). Table 145 presents the frequency and percentage of total tabulations for each category.

Table 145
Frequency and Percentage of
Total Tabulations for Each Category*

Category	Israeli No.	Pct.	Arab No.	Pct.	Total No	Pct.
Aggression	4	2.5	37	22.7	41	25.2
Imperialism	3	1.8	0	0.0	3	1.8
Land legitimacy	14	8.6	4	2.5	18	11.1
Terrorism	0	0.0	3	1.8	3	1.8
Peace seeking	15	9.2	19	11.7	34	20.9
Illegitimacy	1	0.6	0	0.0	1	0.6
Intransigence	12	7.4	16	9.8	28	17.2
Zionism	0	0.0	0	0.0	0	0.0
Action justif.	6	3.7	3	1.8	9	5.5
Culpability	0	0.0	1	0.6	1	0.6
Superpowers					25	15.3

*N = 163.

Table 146, presenting the distribution of the Aggression tabulations, shows that 90 percent were in the area of Arab Aggression.

Table 146
Distribution for
Aggression Tabulations

Aggression Tabulations	Israeli	Arab	Total
Number	4	37	41
Percentage	9.8	90.2	100.0
Tabulations per article	.06	.59	.65
Most in any one day	1	6	

The statements tabulated as Arab Aggression referred to the party who began the war. It is clear that the *Times* perceived the Arab nations as the party which began the conflict.

> It is clear that the Egyptians . . . were determined that this time they would get in their blow first and as far as possible, have the force of surprise on their side ("The Fourth Arab-Israeli War," Oct. 8, 1973).

Although the Arabs are characterized on October 8 as having "bellicose intentions" and Sadat is described as "staging another war," most of the tabulations in this category merely reported the initiation of the conflict. The Israeli Aggression tabulations refer to actions in the 1967 war.

Four of the sixty-three articles (6.4 percent) had at least one tabulation for Israeli Aggression; fifteen (23.8 percent) had at least one for Arab Aggression. Table 147 presents the frequency and percentage of articles in which there was at least one tabulation for each category, showing that Aggression was an important focus of attention for the *Times*.

Table 147
Frequency and Percentage of Editorials
Containing at Least One Tabulation
for Each Category

Category	Israeli No.[a]	Pct.[b]	Arab No.	Pct.	Total No	Pct.
Aggression	4	6.3	15	23.8	15	23.8
Imperialism	3	4.8	0	0.0	3	4.8
Land legitimacy	7	11.1	4	6.3	9	14.3
Terrorism	0	0.0	2	3.1	2	3.1
Peace seeking	8	12.7	9	14.3	13	20.6
Illegitimacy	1	1.6	0	0.0	1	1.6
Intransigence	9	14.3	10	15.9	12	19.0
Zionism	0	0.0	0	0.0	0	0.0
Action justif.	4	6.3	2	3.1	6	9.5
Culpability	0	0.0	1	1.6	1	1.6
Superpowers					14	22.2

[a]Number of editorials with at least one tabulation. There were sixty-three total editorials.
[b]Percentage of total editorial with at least one tabulation.

Imperialism

Only three of the 163 tabulations (1.8 percent) were in the area of Imperialism. Table 148 presents the distribution, showing that all three tabulations refer to purported Israeli policies of expansionism.

**Table 148
Distribution for
Imperialism Tabulations**

Imperialism Tabulations	Israeli	Arab	Total
Number	3	0	3
Percentage	100.0	0.0	100.0
Tabulations per article	.05	0.0	.05
Most in any one day	1	0	

Israel, under David Ben Gurion, is characterized as ". . . extending the boundaries of the new state by first exploiting and then breaking a series of United Nations armistices" ("Israel Must See the Political Realities," Oct. 24, 1973). The Israeli government is described at one point as having a policy that was, to some extent, interested in "the acquisition of territories" ("Europe Ploughs Its Furrow For Peace," Nov. 8, 1973). Three of the sixty-three articles (4.8 percent) had at least one tabulation for Israeli Imperialism.

Land Legitimacy

There were 18 tabulations in this area, which ranked fifth greatest among the categories with 11.1 percent of the total. Table 149 shows that almost 80 percent of the tabulations in this category were in the Israeli column.

Table 149
Distribution for
Land Legitimacy Tabulations

Land Legitimacy Tabulations	Israeli	Arab	Total
Number	14	4	18
Percentage	77.8	22.2	100.0
Tabulations per article	.22	.06	.28
Most in any one day	4	1	

The Israeli Land Legitimacy tabulations were all related to the *Times'* concern for the security of the State of Israel, for example: "It would . . . be a disgraceful failure of the world not to allow a national haven for the Jewish people" ("Britain's Interest in Peace," Oct. 18, 1973). The *Times* of London repeatedly supports an "absolute commitment to the existence of Israel" ("Britain's Self-Interest in the War," Oct. 21, 1973). However, the *Times* considers the occupied areas as land belonging to the Arabs. On October 23, for example, the occupied territory is labeled simply as "Arab land" ("Will Peace Follow Ceasefire?" Oct. 23, 1973). It is harder to pin down a concise policy regarding a Palestinian homeland. On November 28, the *Times* writes:

> The Middle East conflict is in its origins and in its essence a Palestine conflict, and no peace that does not include a settlement of the Palestinian problem is likely to last ("Who Speaks for Palestinians?" Nov. 28, 1973).

The Palestinian problem is perceived as crucial, yet it is unclear as to what type of settlement the newspaper advocates. Seven of the sixty-three articles (11.1 percent) had at least one tabulation for Israeli Land Legitimacy, and four (6.4 percent) at least one for Arab Land Legitimacy.

Terrorism

There were three tabulations in this area, less than 2 percent of the total. Table 150 shows all three in the area of Arab Terrorism.

Table 150
Distribution for
Terrorism Tabulations

Terrorism Tabulations	Israeli	Arab	Total
Number	0	3	3
Percentage	0.0	100.0	100.0
Tabulations per article	0	.05	.05
Most in any one day	0	2	

The statements tabulated in this area were ones labeling members of the Palestinian Liberation Organization as terrorists or guerrillas. There was no condemnation of their activities; they were simply described as guerrillas or as members of a terrorist organization. Terrorism was mentioned in only two of the sixty-three editorials.

Peace Seeking

Peace Seeking ranked second in frequency with thirty-four of the 163 tabulations (20.9 percent. Table 151 shows an almost even distribution of the tabulations.

Table 151
Distribution for
Peace Seeking Tabulations

Peace Seeking Tabulations	Israeli	Arab	Total
Number	15	19	34
Percentage	44.1	55.9	100.0
Tabulations per article	.24	.30	.54
Most in any one day	4	5	

Despite the slightly greater frequency in the Arab category, it was clear that the *Times* of London perceived both parties as making efforts to secure peace. Of the Arabs the newspaper writes, "Their purpose is to get a permanent Middle East peace settlement" ("First and Last Chance for a Real Middle East Peace," Oct. 19, 1973). Of the Israelis, "What Israel has always wanted has been an agreement with her Arab neighbors" ("The Aim Should Still Be Peace," Oct. 11, 1973). Israel is characterized as a country that "will heartily endorse peace aims" ("A Chance for Israel to Seize," Oct. 25, 1973). The *Times* writes of President Sadat, "A reasonable reading of all his actions and statements since he succeeded Nasser three years ago is that he has all along been looking for a peaceful settlement" ("Will Peace Follow Ceasefire?" Oct. 23, 1973). Although there are statements which also indicate the parties' belligerence, it is clear that the *Times* considers both parties to be concerned with peace and its attainment. Nine editorials (14.3 percent) had at least one tabulation for Arab Peace Seeking; eight (12.7 percent) had at least one for Israeli Peace Seeking.

Illegitimacy

There was only one tabulation in the area of Illegitimacy. This was in a statement that referred to the illegitimacy of the Israeli occupation of the territories ("Britain's Self-Interest in the War," Oct. 21, 1973). This is consistent with the attitude expressed in the Land Legitimacy category vis a vis the occupied territories.

Intransigence

Intransigence ranked third among the categories, with 17.2 percent of the total. As Table 152 demonstrates, the *Times* tabulations are evenly distributed.

**Table 152
Distribution for
Intransigence Tabulations**

Intransigence Tabulations	Israeli	Arab	Total
Number	12	16	28
Percentage	42.9	57.1	100.0
Tabulations per article	.19	.25	.44
Most in any one day	3	4	

As in the related category of Peace Seeking, the *Times* considered both parties equally intransigent. Regarding the war, "Neither side shows any sign of wanting to stop. . . . Israel and Egypt both still believe they can win more from the war than the peace" ("Britain's Self-Interest in the War," Oct. 21, 1973). Israel is described as refusing to withdraw to the October 22 ceasefire lines on "somewhat specious ground" ("Common Sense on the Canal Banks," Nov. 10, 1973). The *Times'* comment regarding King Faisal: "Having seen the whole world tremble before his oil weapon, [King Faisal] apparently does not see the need for negotiation at all" ("The Arabs' Negotiation Position," Nov. 29, 1973). Despite a slightly greater tabulation frequency for Arab Intransigence, it was apparent that both parties were perceived as displaying intransigence at various times. Nine of the sixty-three articles (14.3 percent) had at least one tabulation for Israeli Intransigence, and ten (15.9 percent) at least one on the Arab side.

Zionism

There were no tabulations in the category regarding the question of whether Zionism is practical or impractical.

Action Justification

There were only nine tabulations in this area, 5.5 percent of the total. Table 153 shows that two-thirds of the tabulations were in the area of Israeli Action Justification.

Table 153
Distribution for
Action Justification Tabulations

Action Justif. Tabulations	Israeli	Arab	Total
Number	6	3	9
Percentage	66.7	33.3	100.0
Tabulations per article	.10	.05	.15
Most in any one day	2	2	

The statements in the Israeli Action Justification category justified Israel's military endeavors. The *Times* felt that Israel must retain its military superiority: "Israel has never known a day's peace since it was created among the horrors of the Arab invasion let loose by Ernest Bevin" ("Forcing the Peace in the Middle East," Oct. 10, 1973). The opinion of the *Times* was that Israel's military might was necessary to maintain the existence of the State of Israel. The tabulations for Arab Action Justification correspond to statements justifying the alleged Arab offensive in the 1973 war as a move toward expediting an eventual peace: "Cairo . . . started up the war again to give peace negotiations a chance" ("Egypt on the Warpath for the Sake of Peace," Oct. 9, 1973). Four of the articles had a tabulation for Israeli Action Justification, and two mentioned Arab Action Justification.

Culpability

There was only one tabulation in the Culpability category, corresponding to a statement in the first editorial regarding the beginning of the war:

> So once again the Middle East is plunged into large-scale bloodshed and destruction. That is a tragedy for all concerned, and those who took the decision to do it--presumably President Sadat and President Assad--bear a heavy responsibility ("The Fourth Arab-Israeli War," Oct. 8, 1973).

Superpower/International Culpability

Superpower Culpability ranked fourth among the categories, with 15.3 percent of the total. Table 154 presents the distribution.

Table 154
Distribution for Superpower/
International Culpability Tabulations

Superpower Culpability	Total
Number	25
Percentage of total	15.3
Tabulations per article	.40
Most in any one day	4

The *Times* considered the United Nations, the Soviet Union individually, and the superpowers collectively culpable for some portion of the conflict. Table 155 presents the distribution within this category.

Table 155
Distribution for Superpower/ International Culpability Tabulations

Superpower Culpability	Super-powers	United Nations	Soviet Union
Number	16	1	8
Percentage	64.0	4.0	32.0
Tabulations per article	.25	.02	.13

The United Nations Security Council--specifically the Arab sympathizers--were admonished for their lack of interest in peace:

> Those who favor the Arab cause--and they are in the majority--will not lift a finger as long as there seems to be the remotest chance of an Egyptian success. Only if the Israelis were seen to be poised for the occupation of Damascus and an advance towards Cairo would they consent to a call going from New York for a ceasefire ("Forcing the Peace in the Middle East," Oct. 10, 1973).

The Soviets are admonished for their military role, the belated attempt to seek peace, and their role in the oil embargo:

> For this [escalation of the war] the Russians bear the main responsibility ("The Russians Tend the Fire," Oct. 17, 1973).

> Only when the Israelis began to turn the tide did the Soviet Union resume its role as a peacemaker and call Dr. Kissinger urgently to Moscow ("Russia's Two Policies," Oct. 27, 1973).

> The Arabs are getting all the blame for what could be a very cold winter while the Kremlin's backstage role tends to be over-

looked ("Arab Oil Weapon in a Moscow Refinery," Nov. 20, 1973).

Most of the tabulations in this category relate to the culpability of the superpowers as a group. Often, the war is termed a *client* war. The *Times* urges the superpowers to "seek a ceasefire at once rather than each waiting to see how his client performs on the battlefield ("The Aim Should Be Peace," Oct. 11, 1973). The *Times* feels that the superpowers "at least, are very much parties to the conflict" ("The Possible Terms for Peace," Oct. 19, 1973). Late in November, the *Times* writes:

> The recent phase in the Middle East crisis has shown how superpower politics, so far from avoiding a nuclear holocaust, can bring it alarmingly close--and the rest of the world is apparently able to do very little about it . . . the fact is, that a world dominated by superpowers--whether two, three, four, or even five--may be an attractive proposition if you happen to be one of the superpowers. It contains, however, a number of serious and persistent threats to world stability ("Intricacies of the Great Power Military Two Step," Nov. 23, 1973).

There were additional comments not tabulated which convey the paper's displeasure with the role Great Britain was (or was not) playing in the conflict. The *Times* felt that "The official British attitude is odious--but not more odious than usual" (Arabists hold All the Cards at the FO," Oct. 17, 1973). Later that month the *Times* offered a wry assessment of Britain's role in the conflict:

> That the British government on its own had been powerless to affect the course of events in the Middle East is not surprising. Like France, Britain is now a nation state of the second rank and has lost that magic power which alone, to adopt a memorable Americanism, protects one from against the humiliation of being addressed by the rest of the world as, "Hey, you!" . . . The British government's contribution to the crisis was reminiscent of Groucho Marx's description of the food at a well known New York restau-

> rant--unappetizing, and such small portions ("If We Cannot Make Peace, We Can At Least Make Sense," Oct. 26, 1973).

The paper was unhappy with the British refusal to supply arms to either warring party: "Under the portentous rubric of evenhandedness, the supply of arms to Israel was stopped" ("If We Cannot Make Peace, We Can At Least Make Sense," Oct. 26, 1973). Earlier that month, the *Times* had written:

> This claim [to evenhandedness] is almost certainly specious . . . As far as is known Syria has no British weapons at all. Egypt has none of any great strategic significance . . . Israel's sense of injury is highly understandable ("The Russians Tend the Fire," Oct. 17, 1973).

And in the later article:

> To supply a country with weapons of whatever long a period and then to stop doing so as soon as that country is at war, and furthermore, to refuse it spare parts for those weapons, already supplied, can only be described as an incursion into the higher realms of irrationality ("If We Cannot Make Peace, We Can at Least Make Sense," Oct. 26, 1973).

The dissatisfaction of the *Times* with the role of the government, while quite evident, was not on the same level as the statements attributing guilt to the Soviet Union and the superpowers collectively.

Fourteen of the sixty-three articles (22.2 percent) had at least one tabulation in this category.

Part III. The Impact of Oil

Well over half of the tabulations were in the oil category: 305 of the total 468, or 65.2 percent. See Table 156 for the distribution of totals. Although the scope of this category is greater than the others, it is still apparent that the oil issue was a major concern for the *London Times*. Over half of the articles (57.1 percent) had at least one tabulation in this category, and eleven had more than ten statements.

Table 156
Distribution of Total Tabulations
Including the Oil Category*

Category	Number of Tabulations	Percent of Total
Oil	305	65.2
Aggression	41	8.8
Imperialism	3	0.6
Land legitimacy	18	3.8
Terrorism	3	0.6
Peace seeking	34	7.3
Illegitimacy	1	0.2
Intransigence	28	6.0
Zionism	0	0.0
Action justif.	9	1.9
Culpability	-	0.2
Superpowers	25	5.3

*N = 468.

Table 157 presents the distribution of the Oil tabulations over time, while Table 158 presents the distribution of all articles over time.

Table 157
Oil Tabulations Distributed
Over Two Time Periods

Oil Tabulations	Oct. 6 - Nov. 5	Nov. 6 - Dec. 8
Number	104	201
Percentage	34.1	65.9

Table 158
Editorial Frequency Distributed
Over Two Time Periods

Editorials	Oct. 6 - Nov. 5	Nov. 6 - Dec. 8
Number	33	30
Percentage	52.4	47.6

As expected, there were more tabulations for Oil after the economic boycott than there had been before the boycott. Also as expected, there were more articles printed regarding the conflict one month after its outbreak than there were two months after its outbreak. The oil embargo did not affect the editorial position of the newspaper. The *Times* commented, sometimes critically, on the policies of the government vis a vis the embargo, but its perspective regarding the categories did not change. The newspaper remained slightly pro-Israeli throughout the sixty day period of examination. As Tables 159 through 172 indicate, there is nothing to suggest any change in *Times* of London editorial perspective regarding the Middle East conflict as a result of the oil embargo.

Table 159
Aggression Tabulations
Distributed over Two Time Periods

Category	Oct. 6 - Nov. 5 No.[a]	Pct.[b]	Nov. 6 - Dec. 8 No	Pct.
Israeli	3	75.0	1	25.0
Arab	34	91.9	3	8.1
Total	37	90.2	4	9.8

[a]Number of tabulations.
[b]Percentage of tabulations in respective category.

Table 160
Articles in Which at Least One
Aggression Tabulation Occurs
Over Two Time Periods

Category	Oct. 6 - Nov. 5 No.[a]	Pct.[b]	Nov. 6 - Dec. 8 No	Pct.
Israeli	3	9.1	1	3.3
Arab	12	36.4	3	10.0
Total	12	36.4	3	10.0

[a]Number of articles with at least one tabulation.
[b]Percentage of articles with at least one tabulation.

**Table 161
Imperialism Tabulations
Distributed over Two Time Periods**

Category	Oct. 6 - Nov. 5 No.[a]	Pct.[b]	Nov. 6 - Dec. 8 No	Pct.
Israeli	2	66.7	1	33.3
Arab	0	0.0	0	0.0
Total	2	66.7	1	33.3

[a]Number of tabulations.
[b]Percentage of tabulations in respective category.

**Table 162
Imperialism in Which at Least One
Aggression Tabulation Occurs
Over Two Time Periods**

Category	Oct. 6 - Nov. 5 No.[a]	Pct.[b]	Nov. 6 - Dec. 8 No	Pct.
Israeli	2	6.1	1	3.3
Arab	0	0.0	0	0.0
Total	2	6.1	1	3.3

[a]Number of articles with at least one tabulation.
[b]Percentage of articles with at least one tabulation.

Table 163
Land Legitimacy Tabulations
Distributed over Two Time Periods

Category	Oct. 6 - Nov. 5 No.[a]	Pct.[b]	Nov. 6 - Dec. 8 No	Pct.
Israeli	10	71.4	4	28.6
Arab	3	75.0	1	25.0
Total	13	72.2	5	27.8

[a]Number of tabulations.
[b]Percentage of tabulations in respective category.

Table 164
Articles in Which at Least One
Land Legitimacy Tabulation Occurs
Over Two Time Periods

Category	Oct. 6 - Nov. 5 No.[a]	Pct.[b]	Nov. 6 - Dec. 8 No	Pct.
Israeli	5	15.2	2	6.7
Arab	3	9.1	1	3.3
Total	7	21.2	2	6.7

[a]Number of articles with at least one tabulation.
[b]Percentage of articles with at least one tabulation.

Table 165
Terrorism Tabulations
Distributed over Two Time Periods

Category	Oct. 6 - Nov. 5 No.[a]	Pct.[b]	Nov. 6 - Dec. 8 No	Pct.
Israeli	0	0.0	0	0.0
Arab	1	33.3	2	66.7
Total	1	33.3	2	66.7

[a]Number of tabulations.
[b]Percentage of tabulations in respective category.

Table 166
Articles in Which at Least One
Terrorism Tabulation Occurs
Over Two Time Periods

Category	Oct. 6 - Nov. 5 No.[a]	Pct.[b]	Nov. 6 - Dec. 8 No	Pct.
Israeli	0	0.0	0	0.0
Arab	1	3.0	1	3.3
Total	1	3.0	1	3.3

[a]Number of articles with at least one tabulation.
[b]Percentage of articles with at least one tabulation.

Table 167
Peace Seeking Tabulations
Distributed over Two Time Periods

Category	Oct. 6 - Nov. 5 No.[a]	Pct.[b]	Nov. 6 - Dec. 8 No	Pct.
Israeli	13	86.7	2	13.3
Arab	19	100.0	0	0.0
Total	32	94.1	2	5.9

[a]Number of tabulations.
[b]Percentage of tabulations in respective category.

Table 168
Articles in Which at Least One
Peace Seeking Tabulation Occurs
Over Two Time Periods

Category	Oct. 6 - Nov. 5 No.[a]	Pct.[b]	Nov. 6 - Dec. 8 No	Pct.
Israeli	6	18.2	2	6.7
Arab	9	27.3	0	0.0
Total	11	33.3	2	6.7

[a]Number of articles with at least one tabulation.
[b]Percentage of articles with at least one tabulation.

Table 169
Intransigence Tabulations
Distributed over Two Time Periods

Category	Oct. 6 - Nov. 5 No.[a]	Pct.[b]	Nov. 6 - Dec. 8 No	Pct.
Israeli	9	75.0	3	25.0
Arab	9	56.30	7	43.7
Total	18	64.3	10	35.7

[a]Number of tabulations.
[b]Percentage of tabulations in respective category.

Table 170
Articles in Which at Least One
Intransigence Tabulation Occurs
Over Two Time Periods

Category	Oct. 6 - Nov. 5 No.[a]	Pct.[b]	Nov. 6 - Dec. 8 No	Pct.
Israeli	6	18.2	3	10.0
Arab	6	18.2	4	13.3
Total	6	18.2	6	20.0

[a]Number of articles with at least one tabulation.
[b]Percentage of articles with at least one tabulation.

Table 171
Action Justification Tabulations
Distributed over Two Time Periods

Category	Oct. 6 - Nov. 5 No.[a]	Oct. 6 - Nov. 5 Pct.[b]	Nov. 6 - Dec. 8 No	Nov. 6 - Dec. 8 Pct.
Israeli	4	66.7	2	33.3
Arab	3	100.0	0	0.0
Total	7	77.8	2	22.2

[a]Number of tabulations.
[b]Percentage of tabulations in respective category.

Table 172
Articles in Which at Least One
Action Justification Tabulation Occurs
Over Two Time Periods

Category	Oct. 6 - Nov. 5 No.[a]	Oct. 6 - Nov. 5 Pct.[b]	Nov. 6 - Dec. 8 No	Nov. 6 - Dec. 8 Pct.
Israeli	3	9.1	1	3.3
Arab	2	6.1	0	0.0
Total	5	15.2	1	3.3

[a]Number of articles with at least one tabulation.
[b]Percentage of articles with at least one tabulation.

168 Mass Communication and International Politics

Part IV. Summary: The *Times* of London

The *Times* of London had a slightly pro-Israel perspective regarding the Middle East conflict. Table 173 presents the overall tabulations.

Table 173
Overall Tabulations

	Pro-Israeli	Pro-Arab
Aggression	37	4
Imperialism	0	3
Land legitimacy	14	4
Terrorism	3	0
Peace seeking	15	19
Illegitimacy	0	1
Intransigence	16	12
Zionism	0	0
Action justif.	6	3
Culpability	1	0
Total	92	46
Percentage of total	66.7	33.3

There were twice as many pro-Israeli than pro-Arab statements, but it should be noted that thirty-four of the forty-six additional pro-Israeli tabulations were in a single category. The analysis of the *Times* of London editorials reveals the following perceptions:

1. The Arab nations were the aggressors.
2. Israel has extended its boundaries.
3. a. Israel has a right to exist as a state.
   b. The occupied territory belongs to the Arabs.
4. There are Arab terrorist groups.
5. Both Israel and the Arab nations have sought peace.
6. Both Israel and the Arab nations have been intransigent.
7. a. Israel is justified, to some extent, for maintaining her military might.
   b. The Arab nations were justified, to some extent, for starting the war.
8. The Soviet Union and the superpowers as a group were culpable for exacerbating the conflict.

9. British government actions in the conflict were not appropriate.
10. Oil was a pervasive issue of concern but did not affect the paper's perspectives regarding the categories in the war.
11. The oil embargo had no effect on the perceptions of the *Times* of London as expressed in their editorials.

Chapter 9

CONCLUSIONS

The Non-Oil Categories

It is readily apparent that there were perceptual inconsistencies on the purported key issues in the Arab-Israeli conflict. In each of the categories, the results revealed at least a dichotomy in perception.

Aggression

The Arabs were considered the aggressors, at least in the immediate conflict, by the *New York Times, Straits Times, Asahi Evening News,* and *London Times.* The Israelis were seen as the aggressors by the *Moscow News* and the *Daily Graphic.*

Imperialism

The *Moscow News, Daily Graphic, Asahi Evening News,* and *Times* of London perceived the Israelis to be imperialistic. The *Straits Times* and *New York Times* did not describe either the Israelis or the Arabs as imperialistic.

Land Legitimacy

Regarding Israel's right to exist as a nation, only the *Daily Graphic* and *Moscow News* were equivocal; all other papers supported this right. However, the occupied territory was perceived as Arab land by the *Times* of London and *Asahi Evening News* as well as the *Moscow News* and *Daily Graphic.* The *Straits Times* supported Resolution 242, but did not state exactly what is meant by the occupied territory. The *New York Times* felt that Israel should hold on to the territories until a genuine peace existed.

Terrorism

Only the *New York Times* made no comment regarding terrorism. The *Moscow News* and *Daily Graphic* perceived Israel as employing terrorist tactics; the *Straits Times* labeled Israeli acts during the 1948 war as terrorist. The *Asahi Evening News* perceived both parties as employing terrorism. The *Times* of London described members of the PLO as guerrilla warriors or terrorists.

Peace Seeking

While most of the papers acknowledged peace seeking efforts on both sides of the conflict, the Arab nations were perceived by the *Moscow News, Daily Graphic, Asahi Evening News,* and *Straits Times* as making the greater efforts to seek peace. The *New York Times* and *Times* of London felt that both nations made equal efforts to attain peace.

Intransigence

Like Peace Seeking, this was an area in which both sides participated. The *Straits Times* and *Times* of London perceived both parties as more or less equal in this regard. The Arabs were seen as more intransigent by the *New York Times* and *Asahi Evening News,* and the Israelis by the *Moscow News* and *Daily Graphic*.

Zionism

The *Moscow News* and *Daily Graphic* perceived Zionism to be impractical. The other newspapers made no comment regarding Zionism.

Action Justification

The Arabs were perceived as acting justifiably by the *Moscow News, Daily Graphic, Asahi Evening News,* and *Straits Times*. The *Times* of London and the *New York Times* perceived Israel's actions to be justified.

Culpability

In discussing the relative culpability of the Arabs and Israelis, the *Straits Times* and *Asahi Evening News* made no comment. The *New York Times* and *Times* of

London attributed guilt to the Arabs for certain actions, while the *Moscow News* and *Daily Graphic* perceived Israel as culpable.

Superpower/International Culpability

The *Straits Times* and *Asahi Evening News* felt that the culpability really belonged, not with the Arabs or Israelis but with the superpowers. While all the papers assigned blame to the UN, the US, or the USSR, the *New York Times* and *Times* of London considered the Soviet Union the primary guilty party. Predictably, the *Moscow News* and *Daily Graphic* deemed the United States primarily culpable. It was the papers without strong political alliances to either side which offered "a plague on both your houses."

The Oil Issue

None of the newspapers examined altered their editorial positions because of the oil embargo, although the *Asahi Evening News* did devote more space to the conflict once the embargo had been implemented.

The *Times* of London wrote, "This time the Arabs started it. Of this there can be no reasonable doubt" ("The Fourth Arab-Israeli War," Oct. 8, 1973). However, this study has demonstrated that there is doubt, not only among politicians but among news editors who write for large readerships. Unanimity of opinion does not exist on any issue studied herein. This recognition, and its corollary that similar doubts exist in the minds of the people who read these editorials and form their own opinions, is the major value of this particular research.

It is essential in international endeavors to recognize that there is doubt, which may be the stuff of actual differences of opinion, or economic realities, or political orientation. Whatever the reason, the perceptual disparities are real, and they cloud all attempts to communicate. The identification of perceptual differences, particularly in matters with global implications, is an essential first step in any effective communication regarding international relations.

Regarding the Arab-Israeli conflict, it is sadly the case that on both sides there is little recognition of the position of the other side. The conflict is exacerbated when the combatants and their supporters do not allow that the real picture can appear different when seen from a different angle.

There is no attempt here to legitimize any party's actions. Rather, the point here is that if normal diplomatic relationships in the Middle East are genuinely sought, then nations, parties, groups--whatever the collective might be-- need to recognize and identify the perceptual disparities that exist on key issues in the conflict.

Table 174
Tabulation Summary

	NY Times	Moscow News	Straits Times	Daily Graphic	Asahi News	Times of London
Aggression						
Arab	38	0	12	0	3	37
Israeli	6	97	3	16	4	4
Imperialism						
Arab	0	0	0	0	0	0
Israeli	0	28	0	10	6	3
Land Legitimacy						
Arab	1	27	7	7	4	4
Israeli	6	0	7	1	3	14
Terrorism						
Arab	0	0	0	0	4	3
Israeli	0	46	1	3	3	0
Peace Seeking						
Arab	22	9	14	2	3	19
Israeli	21	2	8	0	1	15
Illegitimacy						
Arab	1	0	0	0	0	0
Israeli	0	21	0	10	3	1
Intransigence						
Arab	17	0	5	0	3	16
Israeli	12	44	3	11	1	12
Zionism						
Practical	0	0	0	0	0	0
Impractical	0	4	0	4	0	0
Action Justification						
Arab	0	18	1	5	4	3
Israeli	1	0	0	0	0	6
Culpability						
Arab	1	0	0	0	0	1
Israeli	0	18	0	3	0	0
Superpower/International						
Culpability	47	19	37	8	2	25
Total Tabulations (excluding oil category)	173	333	98	80	68	163
Articles in period which dealt with conflict	68	19	29	7	27	63
Tabulations per article	2.54	17.5	3.31	11.4	2.51	2.58

References

African and Asian Media Survey (1973). London: World Jewish Congress.
AlRoy, Gil Carl (1975), *Behind the Middle East Conflict*. New York: G.P. Putnam and Sons.
Aunery, Uri (1971), *Israel Without Zionism*. New York: Macmillan Co.
Elon, Amos, and S. Hassan (1974), *Between Enemies. A Compassionate Dialogue Between an Israeli and an Arab*. New York: Random House.
Facts on File: Weekly World News Digest (1973), 33: 838-919. New York: Facts on File.
Gervasi, Frank (1967), *The Case for Israel*. New York: Viking.
Goiten, S. D. (1955), *Jews and Arabs*. New York: Schocken Books.
Hadawi, Sami (1969), *The Arab-Israeli Conflict*. Beirut: Institute for Palestinian Studies.
Holsti, O. (1969), *Content Analysis for the Humanities and Social Sciences*. Reading: Addison Wesley.
Kaplan, M. (1957), *System and Process in International Politics*. New York: John Wiley and Sons.
Kaplowitz, N. (1975), "Attitudes of Arab and Israeli Students in the United States Regarding the Arab-Israeli Dispute: A Psychopolitical Study of International Conflict," *Dissertation Abstracts* 35: 7994A.
Khouri, Fred (1968) *The Arab-Israeli Dilemma*. Syracuse: Syracuse University Press.
Lacquer, Walter (1974), *Confrontation: The Middle East and World Politics*. New York: Bantam.
Lilienthal, Alfred (1953), *What Price Israel*. Chicago: H. Regency Co.
Lilienthal, Alfred (1957), *There Goes the Middle East*. New York: Derin-Adai and Co.
London Sunday *Times* Insight Team (1974), *The Yom Kippur War*. New York: Doubleday and Co.
Merrill, J. (1971), *The Foreign Press*. Baton Rouge: Louisiana State University Press.
Pool, I. (1952), *Prestige Papers*. Stanford, CA: Stanford University Press.
Stork, Joe (1975), *Middle East Oil and the Energy Crisis*. New York: Monthly Review Press.
Smith, Arthur (1973), *Transracial Communication*. Englewood Cliffs, NJ: Prentice-Hall, Inc.

Ver Steeg, Clarence (1966), *The Formative Years*. New York: Hill and Wang.
Warburg, James P. (1968), *Crosscurrents in the Middle East*. New York: Atheneum.
Wilcox, Dennis L. (1967), *English Language Newspapers Abroad*. Detroit: Gale Research.

HN 90 .M3 1988

DATE DUE		